THE COMEDIAN AS THE LETTER D:
ERASMUS DARWIN'S COMIC MATERIALISM

ARCHIVES INTERNATIONALES D'HISTOIRE DES IDEES

INTERNATIONAL ARCHIVES OF THE HISTORY OF IDEAS

Series minor

6

DONALD M. HASSLER

THE COMEDIAN AS THE LETTER D:
ERASMUS DARWIN'S COMIC MATERIALISM

THE COMEDIAN AS THE LETTER D: ERASMUS DARWIN'S COMIC MATERIALISM

by

DONALD M. HASSLER

Department of English, Kent State University

MARTINUS NIJHOFF / THE HAGUE / 1973

PRINTED IN THE NETHERLANDS

CONTENTS

PREFACE

The Child is father of the Man;
And I could wish my days to be
Bound each to each by natural piety.

William Wordsworth,
"Ode: Intimations of Immortality"

Wallace Stevens said somewhere that the theory of poetry is the life of poetry.[1] Charles Darwin, who likes poetry, "recognized that at the cost of losing his appreciation of poetry and other things that delighted him in his youth, his mind had become a 'machine for grinding general laws out of large collections of facts.' " [2] Somewhere in between the polar positions of Stevens' extreme aesthetic belief and Darwin's extreme mechanistic belief lies the aesthetics of empirical thought and the whole modern Romantic tradition. There have been men in between who were both mechanists and poets, who both believed in automatic material mechanisms and tried to use the imagination.

Erasmus Darwin was one of these "in between" figures, and since he lived early (1731-1802) in the modern scientific era he was one of the first. This older Darwin, the grandfather of Charles, has not been given due credit as a transitional figure in the development of the literature of our scientific era. Although historically and in terms of intellectual stature the grandfather was a fanciful child compared to the giant grandson, Erasmus Darwin's habits of thought anticipated one of the most distinguishing characteristics of his grandson. (The genetic suggestiveness is fascinating.) Both Darwins loved to theorize and were stubbornly protective of their theories to a point far beyond the usual belief of scientific investigators.[3] The subject of this book is the older Darwin's theorizing – especially his theories about art and literature.

[1] From "Adagia," in Wallace Stevens, *Opus Posthumous*, Samuel French Morse, ed. (New York: Knopf, 1957), p. 178.
[2] Sir Gavin de Beer, *Charles Darwin, A Scientific Biography* (1963; rpt. New York: Anchor Books, 1965), p. 265.
[3] See Peter J. Vorzimmer, *Charles Darwin: The Years of Controversy* (Philadelphia: Temple Univ. Press, 1970). See especially the foreword by Walter F. Cannon.

Darwin's contributions to, or dabblings in, many modern sciences could and should be more fully traced by specialists in those sciences. Darwin was a fascinating, versatile 18th-century *philosophe* – interested in everything. But the dynamics of the vast mechanisms that our ancestors went so far toward unveiling has forced us into greater and greater specialization so that, even though the spirit of my book is, I hope, Darwinian, its method is to focus on the special topic of literature. Even here it would take greater specialization than I am capable of now to explain fully Darwin's relationship to and influence upon his famous literary contemporaries, the first generation Romantics. Wordsworth and Coleridge experienced their great decade of innovation in the same period that Darwin published all of his major work (1789-1803). It is well known that Darwin was one of the *ancien régime* writers that the Romantics reacted against, and Wordsworth seems to single him out in particular for abuse in the *Preface* of 1800. But there are also many similarities between Darwin's theorizing, and even his practice, and what the Romantics found that they had to do with imagination. The student of Romanticism will recognize these similarities and implied influences as I mention them throughout what follows. As far as presenting exhaustive evidence, however, that Wordsworth read and assimilated Darwin's theories, I cannot do that here. I suspect, in fact, that that probably cannot be done. Darwin was simply very much *there* in the 1790s for us to notice if we want to. Wordsworth and Coleridge chose not to notice too much because they were *there* too – competing and sharing.

Darwin was not finally as good a poet, in my judgment, as he was a general thinker or theorizer. This means that we will never cherish and anthologize him as much as we do our complete poets. But one thing that Darwin teaches us is that we can never have the complete poets that we would want, and he also teaches us how to bear it. Wallace Stevens, in our own time, learned this and learned how to bear it. His important poem, "The Comedian as the Letter C," which is borrowed for my title, is about a minor poet's acceptance of his position as a minor poet. Stevens says of his poet:

> He gripped more closely the essential prose
> As being, in a world so falsified,
> The one integrity for him, the one
> Discovery still possible to make,
> To which all poems were incident, unless
> That prose should wear a poem's guise at last.[4]

[4] Wallace Stevens, *Harmonium* (New York: Knopf, 1953), p. 62.

In the organization of this book, Darwin's prose, his ideas and attitudes, are discussed first, and then some more successful snatches of his poetry later. Darwin is a minor poet, even a bad poet in some respects, but his problems are our problems and his existence and survival need to be more fully noted. In a sense that Wordsworth could never really correct, he is a symptom of and plotter of our literature.

CHAPTER ONE

VARIETIES OF DESPAIR

> Yet the quotidian saps philosophers
> And men like Crispin like them in intent,
> If not in will, to track the knaves of thought.

Wallace Stevens,
"The Comedian as the Letter C"

I

In January 1759, Samuel Johnson, London wit and son of Michael Johnson former bookseller and stationer in Lichfield, learned that his mother was suffering probably her final illness. He wrote frequent, compassionate notes to his mother in Lichfield but was unable to come down to see her before her death toward the end of the month. In fact, Johnson had not visited the lacy cathedral town in which he had grown up for twenty years, and when he finally did return in the winter of 1761-62 it must have been a melancholy visit because his subsequent mention of the visit to his friend Joseph Baretti reads with all the pathos of Imlac's despair at his homecoming:

Last winter I went down to my native town, where I found the streets much narrower and shorter than I thought I had left them, inhabited by a new race of people, to whom I was very little known. . . . I wandered about for five days, and took the first convenient opportunity of returning to a place, where, if there is not much happiness, there is, at least, such a diversity of good and evil, that slight vexations do not fix upon the heart. . . .

Moral sentences appear ostentatious and tumid, when they have no greater occasions than the journey of a wit to his own town; yet such pleasures and such pains make up the general mass of life; and as nothing is little to him that feels it with great sensibility, a mind able to see common incidents in their real state, is disposed by very common incidents to very serious contemplations. Let us trust that a time will come, when the present moment shall be no longer irksome; when we shall not borrow all our happiness from hope, which at last is to end in disappointment.[1]

[1] To Mr. Joseph Baretti, At Milan. London, July 20, 1762. In James Boswell, *Life of Johnson* (1791; rpt. London: Oxford University Press, 1904), pp. 263-64. I am indebted to Bertrand H. Bronson for suggesting the similarity between Johnson and Imlac's homecomings and emphasizing the autobiographical nature of the despair in Rasselas. See his "Postscript Rasselas" in *Samuel Johnson, Rasselas, Poems, and Selected Prose* (San Francisco: Rinehart, 1971), pp. xix-xx.

Johnson's moods of black despair, however, were most eloquently expressed in the great work of art that he wrote so quickly during the January of his mother's death. *Rasselas* does not expound a skepticism, of course, of the extreme variety that is a main concern of this book. Johnson always implies that the reader should make the choice of eternity, and this is a long way from the secularism and materialism that I will describe. In fact, Johnson's ferocious and outspoken piety and devotion to Christianity should disqualify him from assuming the initial position in a study of late 18th-century Pyrrhonism, which is the best "ism," I think, to describe Darwin's general philosophic position. But many of the epigrammatic sentences in *Rasselas* express so well the sense of continual balancing and uncertainty, the sense of probabilities, that was the legacy of Newton and Locke to the 18th century that Johnson should in fact lead-off as the best wit of them all:

Every hour, answered the princess, confirms my prejudice in favour of the position so often uttered by the mouth of Imlac, "That nature sets her gifts on the right hand and on the left." Those conditions, which flatter hope and attract desire, are so constituted, that, as we approach one, we recede from another.... Of the blessings set before you make your choice, and be content.[2]

Classic lines about uncertainty written by a wit who, like Pope, wanted his language to be "correct" so that we would remember ideas in his words may serve, then, as the introductory focal point for a discussion of what some critics have recently been calling "sensibility" in 18th-century literature.[3] I prefer to call the attitude or literary stance "comic materialism," however, in order to emphasize its relation to the scientific revolutions of the time as well as the element of psychological defense against the discoveries of science – the "comic" drive to be content. At the time Johnson was purging himself of unhappiness by writing *Rasselas*, three other Britishers who will figure in this discussion were also trying to make their choices for contentment. David Hume, the most famous man of letters in England at the time and the most notorious skeptic, was enjoying the celebrity of his steadily growing *History of England*. Thomas Gray, the best of contemporary poets, was living in London and making lists at the British Museum in order to control his unhappiness. And Erasmus Darwin was just beginning to cultivate his garden in Lichfield – to establish an extremely lucrative and renowned medical practice and to raise a total of fourteen children. Of these four men, Darwin may have been the most content, but he is without question

---

[2] *Rasselas,* chapter XXIX.
[3] I will review the ideas of some of these critics at the end of this chapter.

the least known as a writer. For this reason, and with the others in mind, my book will focus on the little known provincial doctor who was beginning his practice near the dying Sarah Johnson, on his skepticism and on his theory of literature.[4]

The superficial resemblances of Darwin to both Johnson and Hume are intriguing and well worth a glance in this introductory section. All three men were precocious children intellectually and said to be rather awkward physically. All three grew to be extremely heavy largeframed men which accentuated their physical awkwardness. Each of them, probably in part because of his ungainly size, appeared clumsy in what the 18th century called "company." And each of them apparently delivered their polished sentences in an equally clumsy manner – Johnson with his famous convolutions and distortions, Hume with a heavy Scottish lowland accent and atrocious French, and Darwin with a pronounced stutter.[5] Gray can be saved until later for fear of yoking too many heterogeneous ideas by violence together although it is interesting that the year 1759 was one of only two or three years that Gray spent in London. Hume was there then seeing the second part of his *History of England* through the press.[6] And Johnson, of course, seldom left London maintaining that any man who is tired of London is tired of life.

Darwin, however, seldom came to London; and he would not settle there even though after his medical reputation was established he could have moved to London profitably. George III repeatedly said, "Why does not Dr. Darwin come to London? He shall be my physician if he comes." [7]

Even more curious and a significant puzzle to untangle was Darwin's reticence about his literary abilities. He began writing verse early, and his poetic talent was encouraged by his masters at Chesterfield School. In 1750, he and his two older brothers matriculated together at St. John's College, Cambridge. A generation earlier Hume had been a precocious younger brother at Edinburgh matriculating in the same class with his

---

[4] One of Johnson's notes to his mother mentions a favorite prescription of Dr. Darwin's. He writes, "Eat as much as you can." [dated Jan. 16, 1759. One of seven letters inserted in the fourth edition of Boswell's *Life . . .* by Malone.] Darwin believed that abundant eating assured good health, but there is no evidence that the young Dr. Darwin did anything specific for Johnson's ninety year old mother. Probably there was nothing to do.

[5] For Johnson, see Boswell and James L. Clifford, *Young Sam Johnson* (New York: McGraw-Hill, 1955). For Hume, see Ernest C. Mossner, *The Life of David Hume* (Oxford: Clarendon Press, 1970). For Darwin, see my subsequent discussion.

[6] Mossner, pp. 391-92.

[7] Hesketh Pearson, *Doctor Darwin* (New York: Walker & Co., 1963), p. 172.

older brother.[8] Darwin won a scholarship of 16 pounds a year, studied classics, mathematics, and medicine. He continued to write respectable poems, and forty-four years later the *European Magazine* published one of his college pieces, "The Death of Prince Frederick." Rather than an uncertain literary career, however, which both Johnson and Hume had elected, Darwin chose a safer profession and went to Edinburgh University, the leading medical school in England, in 1754. His best friend in Edinburgh, James Keir, who later continued the friendship as a member of the famous Lunar Society of Birmingham and a significant chemist, attests to the literary reputation of the young Darwin: "The classical and literary attainments which he had acquired at Cambridge gave him, when he came to Edinburgh, together with his poetical talents and ready wit, a distinguished superiority among the students there." [9]

After Darwin set up practice in Lichfield, during his 25 years there, and later when he moved his practice and large family to nearby Derby, he continued to have a local, "midlands" reputation as a wit and poet. But he refused to make any play for a London audience or for a genuine literary reputation until 1789 when he published half of *The Botanic Garden*. The poem, published in both parts in 1791, was finally such a success along with his prose medical treatise, *Zoonomia* (1794-96), that by the end of the century Coleridge would call him "the first literary character in Europe." [10] Darwin's reticence and anxiety about his writings continued even after he had made the plunge into the arena of the London booksellers. In fact, as one would suspect, they intensified. He continually claimed that he wrote only for money and that he had delayed publishing a major work so long in order not to damage his medical practice. But comments by two of his close friends belie this guise. Anna Seward, poetess and his first biographer, remarks:

I have often smiled to hear him boast of his "so much money per couplet," conscious, as I was, that it was an artful way of telling us how highly his talents were rated.... Darwin would not have written meanly for any price that folly would have paid him for stooping his muse to her level.

James Keir says, "The works of Dr. Darwin are a more faithful monument and more true mirror of his mind than can be said of those of most

---

[8] Mossner, p. 32 and p. 39. For biographical information on Darwin, I am indebted to Pearson in particular as well as to other shorter biographies by his grandson, Charles Darwin, by Anna Seward, Desmond King-Hele, and James V. Logan all listed in the bibliography.

[9] Pearson, pp. 4-5.

[10] To John Thelwall, Feb. 6, 1797. In Earl Leslie Griggs, ed., *Collected Letters of Samuel Taylor Coleridge* (Oxford: Clarendon Press, 1956), I, 305.

authors. He was not one of those who wrote . . . from any other incitement than the ardent love of the subject." [11]

If the reader is, or possibly by the end of this book should become, familiar with Darwin's writing, both poetry and prose, it must seem strange to hear him praised for his "sincerity." From Coleridge right down to the present writer, it has seemed the most obvious common sense and in fact a moral obligation to point out Darwin's artificiality, false glitter, and general evasive insincerity. I will spend a good bit of time in later chapters documenting these qualities. The other alternative, which many have followed, is to ignore Darwin all together because of these unseemly qualities. The young Coleridge talked with Darwin in 1796 at his home in Derby, and was probably chided for his religion. He reports to a friend, "Dr. Darwin [thinks] sincerity a folly and therefore vicious. Your atheistic brethren square their moral systems exactly according to their inclinations. . . . polite and goodnatured [Dr. Darwin is willing] to attain at good by attainable roads." [12] Throughout his letters of this period, Coleridge is troubled by the moral pragmatism of "atheists" and "materialists," just as Wordsworth is suffering more profoundly through the crisis, finally to yield up "moral questions in despair." Sincerity, as well as contented self-confidence about one's literary efforts, are neither one easily attainable as the nervous vitality of *The Prelude* demonstrates. David Perkins' superb recent study of Wordsworth shows how complex the problem of sincerity in literature can become.[13] In view of this growing interest in the problem of sincerity in late 18th-century literature, Darwin's evasions and self-defenses about his literary intentions are simply unexplored territories that we are not too surprised to find. To use an appropriate metaphor for this family of biologists, we can only hope the flora and fauna will be interesting and instructive to study.

Dr. Darwin himself was a shrewd psychologist, in many ways one of the founders of modern psychosomatic theory, and he undoubtedly observed his own evasions and defenses. Anna Seward recalls, "The Doctor was accustomed to remark, that whenever a strange step had been taken, if any way obnoxious to censure, the alleged reason was scarcely ever the real motive." [14] There must have been something scary, then, potentially "obnoxious to censure" about publishing major literary

---

[11] Both quotations are found in Pearson, p. 161.

[12] To John Thelwell. May 13, 1796. In Griggs, I, 214.

[13] David Perkins, *Wordsworth and the Poetry of Sincerity* (Cambridge: Harvard Univ. Press, 1964).

[14] Anna Seward, *Memoirs of the Life of Dr. Darwin* (London: J. Johnson, 1804), p. 169.

works because Darwin delayed so long and then equivocated about his motives when he did publish. We know this, though. Every modern man who has tried "to publish" knows this fear. Since Pope reminded us that epic heroes like Sarpedon were not self-conscious and could act directly and "heroically," we have been self-conscious. And this despairing reticence and uncertainty about what we do, which is really an uncertainty about who we are, may be the great unstated subject matter of modern literature.

An essay, later a book, by Walter Jackson Bate, which should be widely known, makes this point about modern literature with the elegant self-confidence of the historian who can report on uncertainty with certainty. Possibly the detached and incisive reporting of the "investigator," which was David Hume's *métier*, is the only literary genre that can be performed in modern times with contentment. And possibly this is another way of explaining why Darwin remained an investigator so long (publishing papers in the *Transactions* of the Royal Society, sharing in the investigations of the Lunar Society) before he set up as a "poet." In any case, Bate describes a dilemma that reminds us of the speech of the poor princess in *Rasselas*:

The essence of neurosis is conflict. It becomes especially so when you face obviously conflicting demands: when the pressures (or what we imagine the pressures to be) are ones that enjoin us to move in two different — in fact, two *opposing* — directions at once. And what do you do then? I think of the fable of the donkey that starved when he was confronted, on each side, with two equally distant bales of hay. The arts stutter, stagger, pull back into paralysis and indecision before such a conflict of demand.[15]

In addition to the delays, the reticence about motive, and the almost militant provincialism that I have already noticed in Darwin, one or two more personality traits need mention here before we look more fully for the cause. Again, Anna Seward gives the best description:

Conscious of great native elevation above the general standard of intellect, he became, early in life, sore upon opposition, whether in argument or conduct, and always revenged it by sarcasm of very keen edge.... Perhaps this proneness to suspicion mingled too much of art in his wisdom.... Though Dr. Darwin's hesitation in speaking precluded his flow of colloquial eloquence, it did not impede,

---

[15] W. J. Bate, "The English Poet and the Burden of the Past, 1660-1820," in Earl R. Wasserman, ed., *Aspects of the Eighteenth Century* (Baltimore: Johns Hopkins Press, 1965), pp. 263-64. I have not yet seen Bate's book of the same time title reversed (Harvard University Press, 1970), but the reviews I have seen say that it is an elaboration of the argument described here. In any case, my references here are based on my reading of the essay.

or at all lessen, the force of that conciser quality, *wit*. Of satiric wit he possessed a very peculiar species.[16]

His stammer, his caustic sarcasm, his deliberate artificiality of manner were all signs of what Elizabeth Schneider describes so well in Coleridge as the conflict between the awareness of exceptional powers and the awareness of impotence.[17] This conflict is exactly the conflict of the modern writer, as Bate interprets it. He knows that he is, or should be, a writer but he knows that, compared to past writers, he cannot be. In short, he knows too much. In Darwin's particular case, the problem of his stammer illustrates the dilemma well. He could accurately describe the psychology of the stammerer, in the *Zoonomia*, but he could never cure himself (possibly for the very reason that he knew the accurate description):

On this circumstance [trying too hard] depends the impediment of speech before mentioned; the first syllable of a word is causable by volition, but the remainder of it is in common conversation introduced by its association with this first syllable acquired by long habit. Hence when the mind of the stammerer is vehemently employed on some idea of ambition of shining, or fear of not succeeding, the associations of the motions of the muscles of articulation with each other become dissevered by this greater exertion, and he endeavours in vain by voluntary efforts to rejoin the broken associations.[18]

The stammerer cannot relax and let himself stammer, in which case he might improve. He has to try, quite humanly, not to stammer, which makes him stammer. Similarly, the modern writer cannot relax and write. He feels continual uncertainty because he knows so much literature. He then turns, as Bate argues, to sincerity or glittering novelty in order to "shine."

Darwin's glitter and interest in novelty will be the topic of later chapters. The question is, in Darwin's case, when did the uncertainty begin and exactly what was the uncertainty. Bate, as I said, is provocative, the best that I have read on the literary dilemma in Darwin's time and in our own. But Darwin is hardly a major literary figure, and this is partly due to his own choice, as I suggested. So his uncertainty goes beyond, or possibly precedes, the uncertainty of major writers such as Johnson or Wordsworth. Darwin chose during his college years to wrestle with life, not with literature. He probably thought of himself, at least until 1789, primarily as a doctor, a "man of action," and a natural philosopher, a

---

[16] Seward, pp. 2-4, 77.

[17] Elizabeth Schneider, *Coleridge, Opium and Kubla Khan* (Chicago: University of Chicago Press, 1953), pp. 108-09.

[18] Erasmus Darwin, *Zoonomia, or, The Laws of Organic Life* (London: J. Johnson, 1794), I, 193.

"seeker of truth." Why? Why did he wait so long to make a bid for himself as a modern Pope, or a modern Lucretius (he was good, as we shall see, with the heroic couplet, and he was good with the scientific-didactic poem)? Bate emphasizes the pressure of past literature in lowering the sights of writers like Darwin. But I think Bate fails to emphasize enough the positive value of an early-acquired and comprehensive skepticism to transform a mere literary man dealing with the delusions of the gods into a real man wrestling with uncertainties and skeptical after truth. One of David Hume's great *bon mots* applies well here: "Be a philosopher; but amidst all your philosophy, be still a man." [19] Strangely enough we remember Darwin primarily as a man and that almost by default because we know he was neither a great philosopher, nor a great scientist, nor a great poet. But he was all of these things by virtue of his skepticism.

II

Although there is no conclusive evidence, I believe that Darwin's skepticism began when he read mathematics at Cambridge (in the same college where Wordsworth read mathematics forty years later) and that it reached full growth while he was studying in Edinburgh. I believe that he must have read Hume's *Enquiry* this early and that it influenced his thinking. Darwin indicates in the *Zoonomia* much later that he has read and essentially agrees with the *Dialogues*. But I think Hume was in his mind much earlier, along with Newton and Locke, and that these "ideas" are formative in establishing his reticence and his skepticism after truth. The propaganda of our predominantly Christian society tends to slander and bedevil anyone who would raise serious questions about dogma, and following the lead of the prevailing opinion we are more than ready to think of religious skeptics like Hume and Darwin as cocksure, devilish people. But more often than not, a questioner of religious notions begins as a serious, pious young person. Matters of faith and personal conduct mean much to these people. They want to know what they are about. We think of Martin Luther, James Joyce, and even Jesus of Nazareth. Similarly, we are told Hume took "his religion unusually seriously," as a young man: "The boy David Hume was, it is clear, already beginning to think for himself and to deem moral issues of paramount importance." [20]

---

[19] Mossner takes these words as the keynote to his superb biography of Hume and quotes them on the title page.

[20] Mossner, p. 34.

Darwin's biographer describes him also as a serious child, not much interested in casual "pastimes," and quotes a very interesting letter written from Edinburgh in which Darwin evidences his religion but also what sounds like nearly a Humean interest in the probabilities for its validity:

Yesterday's post brought me the disagreeable news of my father's departure out of this sinful world. . . .

He was 72 years old, and died the 20th of this current November 1754. "Blessed are they that die in the Lord."

That there exists a superior *ens entium*, which formed these wonderful creatures, is a mathematical demonstration. That He influences things by a particular providence, is not so evident. The probability, according to my notion, is against it, since general laws seem sufficient for that end. Shall we say no particular providence is necessary to roll this Planet round the Sun, and yet affirm it necessary in turning up *cinque* and *quatorze*, while shaking a box of dice or giving each his daily bread? The light of Nature affords us not a single argument for a future state; this is the only one, that it is possible with God, since He who made us out of nothing can surely re-create us; and that He will do this is what we humbly hope. . . .[21]

Living as a student in Edinburgh with acknowledged literary talent and wit among his fellows, as James Keir told us, Darwin would have had inducements at least to look into the writings of Hume, who was getting a lot of publicity in his native Scotland, both favorable and unfavorable, by 1754. The two most notorious pieces by Hume were two sections on Christianity first published as Section X ("Of Miracles") and Section XI ("Of the Practical Consequences of Natural Religion") of *Philosophical Essays concerning Human Understanding* (later entitled the *Enquiry*) in 1748. The first section had been written ten years earlier to go in *The Treatise,* but Hume was very cautious of the temper of his age (as was Darwin) and had suppressed "Of Miracles" until his literary reputation was more firmly established.[22] Several ideas and phrases in Darwin's youthful letter remind me of particular echoes as well as the overall tenor of argument in Hume's iconoclastic pieces. First of all, Darwin's confidence that "mathematical demonstration" is sufficient recalls Hume's early ambition to become the Newton of human nature, and the notion of "probability" as the determining factor in a conflict is the key notion in "Of Miracles." It is much more probable, Hume argues, that men can be deceived, and deceive, than that miracles occur. Secondly, Darwin's skepticism about "a particular providence" and his belief in "general laws" constitutes a faint echo of the whole drift of Hume's

[21] To Dr. Okes, of Exeter. In Person, pp. 5-6.
[22] See Mossner, pp. 286-288.

Section XI, which, in fact, was later called "Of a Particular Providence and of a Future State." Hume insists over and over in that piece that we must not infer specific characteristics from nature beyond what we experience. If we do not experience "particular" causation, then we must not infer it. If we do not experience a future state, we must not infer it.

Hume's emphasis upon paying close attention to experience and upon seriously trying to weigh the probabilities in all situations produces some very droll observations. He refers to our love of gossip in "Of Miracles," calls it "our natural way of thinking," and continues:

For instance: There is no kind of report, which rises so easily, and spreads so quickly, especially in country places and provincial towns, as those concerning marriages; insomuch that two young persons of equal condition never see each other twice, but the whole neighborhood immediately join them together. The pleasure of telling a piece of news so interesting, of propagating it, and of being the first reporters of it, spreads the intelligence.... Do not the same passions, and others still stronger, incline the generality of mankind to believe and report, with the greatest vehemence and assurance, all religious miracles? 23

If Darwin did read the early essays of Hume, he must have begun to think of everyday serious matters in terms of the mathematics of probability and he would have recognized in the hard-headed Scot a kindred spirit, possibly a teacher of skepticism. At least, we know that the serious, religious young man became educated somewhere to the awareness that there is a high probability that people will deceive you, and themselves, in some situations: "Extreme was his skepticism to human truth. From that cause he often disregarded the accounts his patients gave of themselves." 24

One final idea from Darwin's youthful letter on his father's death is important because it anticipates a later important reference to Hume in Darwin's writings. This is the idea, held by the twenty-three year old Darwin, that God "made us out of nothing." Many years later, in the *Zoonomia*, amidst his fascinating speculations about biological evolution, Darwin writes:

The late Mr. David Hume, in his posthumous works, places the powers of generation much above those of our boasted reason; and adds, that reason can only make a machine, as a clock or a ship, but the power of generation makes the maker of the machine; and probably from having observed, that the greatest part of the earth has been formed out of organic recrements; as the immense beds of

23 David Hume, *An Enquiry Concerning Human Understanding* in Ralph Cohen, ed., *Essential Works of David Hume* (New York: Bantam Books, 1965), p. 131.
24 Seward, p. 3.

limestone, chalk, marble, from the shells of fish; and the extensive provinces of clay, sandstone, ironstone, coals, from decomposed vegetables; all which have been first produced by generation, or by the secretions of organic life; he concludes that the world itself might have been generated, rather than created; that is, it might have been gradually produced from very small beginnings, increasing by the activity of its inherent principles, rather than by a sudden evolution [the word meant in the 18th century "preformation," "creation"] of the whole by the Almighty fiat.[25]

Thus by the end of his career, when he finally mentions Hume (and the reference is to the posthumous *Dialogues concerning Natural Religion*, 1779), Darwin no longer believes in the medieval notion of something from nothing. In between in Darwin's thinking must lie the influence of the full force of British empirical philosophy of the 18th century, and of a skepticism not only about "human truth" (gossip) but about all kinds of knowledge.

The Newtonian-Lockean-Humean skepticism was a deliberate change in the methodology of thinking (epistemology) in order to reap certain results. Skepticism, withheld judgment, was useful because it allowed for the accumulation of information. Furthermore, the model of continually accumulating information, of every growing complex idea, was a good model for the wide-open universe that the new physics and astronomy was theorizing about. Actually, both Lockean epistemology and Newtonian math-physics generally worked from the larger (complex ideas, motions) to the smaller components (simple ideas, forces); but by implication the relationships and sizes could extend to infinity in either direction. This vision of a wide-open universe eventually got into poetry with Wordsworth, and possibly with Darwin.[26] The efficacy of the new methodology was simply the efficacy of analysis – empirical if the objects could be sensed but still analytic even if the objects were too small to be sensed. Locke suggested that the way to understand any large unit (complex idea) is to divide it (analyze it) into smaller units (simple ideas). If something were not analyzable, then it was simply not an object for understanding. The implication, of course, is that all important things – all things that exist – are analyzable. Thus ultimate particles (non-analyzable things) are either not important or, worse, do not exist.

The skeptical implications of this rigorously analytic program for thinking haunted the 18th century. Locke himself always maintained that ultimate particles did exist. He called them primary qualities. And Newton, from whose mathematical method Locke's epistemology derives,

[25] Darwin, *Zoonomia,* I, 509.
[26] For Wordsworth, see Geoffrey Durrant, *Wordsworth and the Great System* (New York: Cambridge U.P., 1970).

always "believed in" ultimate material substance. The important thing is that the method of problem solving for both men neither required that the ultimate particles be dealt with nor, in fact, had any way of dealing with them. The ultimate particles were always a receding will-o-the-wisp in Lockean epistemology or Newtonian math-physics. And it was better that they should be because the analytic method would grind to a halt if there were nothing to analyze.

The theory of matter implied by Newton's writings that was a major source for Locke's epistemology and that Newton's disciples puzzled over throughout the 18th century is a beautifully skeptical theory. We cannot really sample Newton's math, his calculus, which was a way of pinpointing what continually changes (a paradox equally as puzzling as the paradox of analyzing toward ultimate particles that can never be reached); but we can sample his prose. Locke himself was ". . . the first who became a Newtonian Philosopher without the help of [math]" [27] Darwin, of course, studied the mathematics; but what is important for our purposes is to understand the implications of Newton's "mathematical way" for Darwin. Now and then in his writings, Newton would pause to explain how little "ultimate reality" he actually knew, how far he was from calculating anything about ultimate particles. This was particularly effective rhetorically coming from Newton because his math was predicting the motions of very small particles indeed that one would think were very near to ultimate particles. A typical passage is at the end of his masterly measurement of light "corpuscles," which he insists must be material:

In these Descriptions I have been the more particular because it is not impossible but that Microscopes may at length be improved to the discovery of the Particles of Bodies on which their Colours depend, if they are not already in some measure arrived to that degree of perfection. For if those Instruments are or can be so far improved as with sufficient distinctness to represent Objects five or six hundred times bigger than at a Foot distance they appear to our naked Eyes, I should hope that we might be able to discover some of the greatest of those Corpuscles. And by one that would magnify three or four thousand times perhaps they might all be discover'd, but those which produce blackness [i.e. the smallest]. In the mean while I see nothing material in this Discourse that may rationally be doubted of, excepting [accepting] this Position: That transparent Corpuscles of

    [27] I. Bernard Cohen, *Franklin and Newton* (Philadelphia: American Philosophical Society, 1956), p. 123. I am indebted to two other fascinating books and a doctoral dissertation for helping me begin to unravel the mysteries of Newton: Robert E. Schofield, *Mechanism and Materialism, British Natural Philosophy in an Age of Reason* (Princeton: Univ. Press, 1970). Charles Coulston Gillispie, *The Edge of Objectivity, An Essay in the History of Scientific Ideas* (Princeton: Princeton Univ. Press, 1960). Donald D. Ault, *Visionary Physics: Blake's Response to Newton,* Diss. University of Chicago, 1970.

the same thickness and density with a Plate, do exhibit the same Colour. . . . it will add much to our Satisfaction, if those Corpuscles can be discover'd with Microscopes; which if we shall at length attain to, I fear it will be the utmost improvement of this Sense. For it seems impossible to see the more secret and noble Works of Nature within the Corpuscles by reason of their transparency.[28]

The success of Newton's method encouraged many disciples. One of the most talented was Benjamin Franklin, whom Darwin corresponded with often on scientific matters. According to modern students of Franklin, he went much further toward a stated skepticism about ultimate particles than Newton did. Franklin was simply impatient with any consideration of ultimate particles. They probably did not exist, he thought. At least, they could not explain anything. "Franklin did not envisage any stage in which an ultimate cause would be found as a principle within a principle to explain its apparent repulsion of a like particle [rather smaller particles always explained the motion of larger ones]. There would always remain an ultimate unknowable." [29]

When this skeptical theory of matter was broadened in men's minds to become a theory of reality, as it must if it were to be taken seriously, then the ancient and medieval belief in a final and divine purpose in reality was severely shaken. A recent book by a Jesuit, Father John Boyd, sets out to discuss literary theory but lapses into a somewhat anachronistic 20th-century lament for the 18th century loss of faith in final purpose. Father Boyd claims what went wrong was that 18th-century thinkers fell victim to what he calls "univocal" habits of thought. They tried to apply the same methods of analysis to all problems so that when physics revealed illusive ultimate particles, it was assumed that matter itself was infinitely divisable and not simply and humanly knowable. Father Boyd, in fact, writes a good exposition of the methodology which he abhors:

When this spirit [analysis] spread to their thought about God and man, the West experienced a profound shock from which it is still trying to recover. A sense of finality secured the needed sense of transcendence spoken of before. A changing universe without a sense of purpose easily became a desert, man a hopeless wanderer in it, and God little more than a processor of sand.[30]

Many Christians at that time, like Father Boyd today, maintained their religion even though they may have worked in a sophisticated way with

[28] Sir Isaac Newton, *Opticks*, I. Bernard Cohen, ed. Fourth edition (1730; rpt. New York: Dover, 1952), pp. 261-62.
    [29] Cohen, *Franklin and Newton*, pp. 347-48.
    [30] John D. Boyd, S.J., *The Function of Mimesis and Its Decline* (Cambridge: Harvard Univ. Press, 1968), p. 87.

analysis and Newtonian math. Joseph Priestley, scientist and clergyman and a good friend of Darwin's in the Lunar Society, was one. In his *Memoirs,* he describes his attempt to save Benjamin Franklin's religion:

It is much to be lamented that a man of Dr. Franklin's general good character and great influence should have been an unbeliever in Christianity, and also have done so much as he did to make others unbelievers. To me, however, he acknowledged that he had not given so much attention as he ought to have done to the evidences of Christianity, and desired me to recommend to him a few treatises on the subject, such as I thought most deserving of his notice, but not of great length, promising to read them, and give me his sentiments on them. Accordingly, I recommended to him Hartley's evidences of Christianity in his *Observations on Man,* and what I had then written on the subject in my Institutes of Natural and Revealed Religion.[31]

David Hartley would not have been much help in restoring anyone's sense of an anthropomorphic religion because in his writings God becomes a kind of digital accumulation of all complex ideas.[32] In any case, the evidence is strong that Darwin himself lost most of his faith in a personal God, due probably to reading mathematics and possibly to reading Hume on Christianity as well. Towards the end of his life, Darwin had a reputation for mocking Christians. He is reported to have said to Priestley, who was a Unitarian minister, "Unitarianism is a feather-bed to catch a falling Christian." [33]

III

The homogeneous, or to use Father Boyd's phrase, the "univocal" world view derived from Newton, Locke, and Hume that dominated Darwin's serious speculations is the most dramatic and demonstrable source of his skepticism. Newton's "mathematical way" is skepticism. No final answer or final purpose can be found, or is even desired, as that would end "the way." We will return in the next chapter to a fuller description of Darwin's serious speculation as the analyzable basis of his aesthetics and literary intentions. But the mood or precondition of despair, which is the topic of this chapter, and which pervades the literature of sensibility in the second half of the 18th century, is not merely a product of philosophic theory. In many cases, there seemed to be personal, tempera-

[31] Joseph Priestley, *Memoirs,* edited and abriged by John T. Boyer (Washington: Barcroft Press, 1964), p. 77.
[32] For a discussion of Hartley's view of God, see my paper "Belief and Death in Wordsworth's *Peter Bell*" forthcoming in the *Bulletin of the New York Public Library.*
[33] Pearson, p. 120.

mental, even social reasons for despair. Perhaps these were symptoms of the general philosophic skepticism. But the personal problem of the crisis of confidence is worth looking at before we return to philosophy.

"Perhaps no generation of English poets has ever been more aware of its own impermanence, more oppressed by the burden of the past, more self-conscious, more inhibited...." [34] This is Bate's argument about poetic reticence that we glanced at earlier, and the oppression seems to be the rather superficial problem of literary ambition. But this is not really a superficial problem if we consider the propaganda weight of the "poetic mission" – even for our own time. It means a great deal to want to be a poet when we know that it is no longer possible in the "bardic" or Shakespearean sense. Similarly, the anthropomorphic images of a Michelangelo God mean a great deal when we know they are analyzable sensations and have no final validity beyond that. I think we need to emphasize the personal tension implicit in these rather schematic dilemmas already mentioned – particularly the dilemma of knowing literature and thus not being able to write.

Gray was the best poet of the four writers we are interested in here (Hume frankly and wisely said that he was not a poet), and Gray was a reticent poet, writing very little and publishing reluctantly. In 1765, he advised James Beattie, an aspiring poet of Darwin's generation some twenty years younger than Gray himself, not to stake his hopes on poetry, at least not on a poetry that one could be confident about:

> ... you took me too literally, if you thought I meant in the least to discourage you in your pursuit of poetry: all I intended to say was, that if either vanity ... or interest, or ambition has any place in the breast of a poet, he stands a great chance in these our days of being severely disappointed; and yet, after all these passions are suppressed, there may remain in the mind of one ... incitements of a better sort, strong enough to make him write verse all his life, both for his own pleasure and that of all posterity.[35]

For social and economic reasons, as well as psychological, poetry began to "suppress' itself, to become an almost secret and hesitant avocation at the same time that it became a profession paying for itself. Ironically, when the literary profession freed itself of the patron and became commercial and self-supporting, this contributed to the crisis of confidence Bate describes; and the two developments cooperated and complimented

---

[34] Lawrence Lipking, *The Ordering of the Arts in Eighteenth-Century England* (Princeton: Princeton Univ. Press, 1970), p. 377.

[35] To Mr. Beattie, Oct. 2, 1765. Thomas Gray, *Gray's Poems Letters and Essays*, John Drinkwater and Lewis Gibbs, eds. (New York: Dutton, Everyman, 1912), p. 274.

each other enough to produce personal tensions and the "mixed emotions" that we still associate with the role of the poet.

This was a national condition, of course. Gray cloistered himself at Cambridge where Darwin himself may have been one of the under-graduates who teased him in the early 1750s. Scotland had its hesitant bards such as Beattie whom Gray advised to suppress his passions. But no provincial town better illustrates the dilemma of the reticent modern poet than Lichfield where Darwin lived and where Johnson had grown up. From Boswell on we have admired Doctor Johnson for his defiant, sometimes bombastic, refusal to succumb to any crisis of confidence. A deep reading of Johnson's defiance, however, communicates these crises in their most effective form perhaps. For example, Johnson's firm "belief" in a life after death never really convinced Boswell who was always suffering that crisis of confidence nervously.[36] Similarly, Johnson defiantly made his way as a writer, and it should be noted that this was not primarily as a poet. He was a writer. He made his living as a writer. There could be no visible lack of confidence although the despair of Imlac at ever being the poet he would like to be is, of course, Johnson's despair. The effect of this success and confidence must have been devas-tating to Johnson's hometown.

Actually, the painful effects of the hometown boy making good in the big world work both ways. The people of Lichfield during the 50s, 60s and 70s worked very hard to give the impression of ignoring Sam John-son, the son of the bookseller, and to establish their own society. They gossiped about his poor origin, about his marriage to Tetty, about his dogmatism and bad manners. But more significantly, I think, they must have felt compelled to solidify their own gains. Darwin, in particular, had a continual reminder in Johnson of the imperiousness and competi-tiveness of the London world. And, if Darwin had originally decided to pursue a "safe" profession rather than aim his sights at Olympian heights, Johnson's infrequent but triumphant visits to Lichfield must have convinced him that he had been wise to work within a limited context toward attainable goals. This catty history of little Lichfield's relations with the Great Cham is told in part in Margaret Ashmun's book on Anna Seward, and the following passage includes Darwin in the circle of local talent carefully defending their status against the threat of the big world and Johnson:

The Seward girls were growing up to be handsome misses – the elder, a precocious poetess, praised and encouraged by the rising young physician, Dr. Erasmus

---

[36] See Mossner's narrative of Boswell's anxious visits to the dying Hume. Mossner, pp. 597-98.

Darwin. Johnson, in process of becoming the dean and tyrant of British letters, heard of the happy hospitable life of the Sewards, or saw the members of the family themselves on his infrequent visits to his birthplace. The Rev. Mr. Seward, whose memory had not yet failed him, carefully refrained from appearing dazzled by the tardily achieved glories of Michael Johnson's son.[37]

Doctor Darwin was without question the towering intellect in this society of cathedral divines (strangely enough Hume also had many friends among the clergy), literary ladies, and busy amateur scientists. He was a contributing Fellow of the Royal Society, the founder of a provincial scientific society, the Lunar Society, that historians have acknowledged as truly remarkable, and was cultivating a voluminous quantity of his own writing.[38] Undoubtedly, he was good, but Johnson was from a larger arena with more notoriety. The resulting tension must have spurred them both with the awareness that finally there is no arena to satisfy our "passions," as Gray said, enough. It spurred them with despair:

Dr. Johnson was several times at Lichfield ... while Dr. Darwin was one of its inhabitants. They had one or two interviews, but never afterwards sought each other.... Where Dr. Johnson was, Dr. Darwin had no chance of being heard, though at least his equal in genius, his superior in science; nor indeed, from his impeded utterance, in the company of *any* overbearing declaimer; and he was too intellectually great to be an humble listener to Johnson, therefore he shunned him.[39]

This relationship of Johnson and Darwin, then, illustrates in microcosm the burden of literary competition in the present.

Perhaps also the despair of these men was simply the result of the most clear-sighted vision yet of the competitiveness, the "motion" to use Newton's favorite word, of an infinite universe. There was a kind of madness, epidemic in the 18th century, associated with insight and genius. It was a little more intense than the melancholy of the "vapors" or "The English Malady" that Dr. Cheyne described, and that caused many 18th-century women to go into sudden "decline." E. C. Mossner, Hume's biographer, calls it the "disease of the learned" and devotes a chapter to it because Hume suffered severely from it during a four year period immediately after he had finished college and while he was doing intensive independent reading to prepare himself for the life of letters. It is significant that Hume's deliberate decision after finishing college

[37] Margaret Ashmun, *The Singing Swan, An Account of Anna Seward and Her Acquaintance with Dr. Johnson, Boswell, & Others of Their Time* (1931; rpt. New York: Greenwood Press, 1968), p. 116.
[38] For the best account of The Lunar Society see Robert E. Schofield, *The Lunar Society of Birmingham* (Oxford: Oxford University Press, 1963).
[39] Pearson, pp. 19-20. Anna Seward is speaking.

was not to follow a practical and secure profession. There were many lawyers in his family, and he could have had a comfortable career in that profession. But he chose to read instead so that eventually he could extend Newton's methodology into the study of human nature; and he developed severe psychosomatic, hypochondriac symptoms. He was very nervous for a few years as he first looked into the infinite universe.[40]

Characteristic of the strange analogies and counter-analogies linking these four 18th-century writers into the pervasive mood of despair, Johnson suffered from the disease of the learned at nearly the same time Hume did. In the well known passage from the Life, Boswell dismisses the complaint as "The English Malady," but despite his protestations to the contrary Johnson was too clearly aware of the infinite universe to be secure in a mere ladies' disease of nerves. Boswell assigns the onset of Johnson's melancholy to the same summer that Hume, in Scotland, began to notice similar signs of nervousness:

The "morbid melancholy," which was lurking in his constitution, and to which we may ascribe those particularities, and that aversion to regular life, which at a very early period marked his character, gathered such strength in his twentieth year, as to afflict him in a dreadful manner. While he was at Lichfield, in the college vacation of the year 1729, he felt himself overwhelmed with a horrible hypochondria, with perpetual irritation, fretfulness, and impatience; and with a dejection, gloom, and despair, which made existence misery. From this dismal malady he never afterward was perfectly relieved; and all his labours, and all his enjoyments, were but temporary interruptions of its baleful influence.[41]

Hume recovered from the melancholy probably because he fully accepted the half-knowledge and relativism of the analytic method that he was helping to establish. Johnson never did recover completely because he defiantly refused to accept such half-knowledge. But Darwin, our main interest here, seems to have instinctively avoided the melancholy altogether by practical and limited hard work from the time he left college. As we noticed earlier, Darwin's decision to pursue an established profession, which neither Johnson, Hume, nor Gray did, is significant for several reasons. It is probably the mark of his lesser, grand human accomplishment. But it is also the reason for a vast quantity of accumulative acts and ideas that were effective at the time and that have been passed on into the stream of subsequent human accomplishments without the unified glory of a great name, but with the validity of tentative, accumulating, Lockean data. Darwin was a good company man for the

---

[40] Mossner, pp. 66 ff. Michel Foucault's book *Madness and Civilization* is about the nervous disease of the 18th century, but I have not seen it.
[41] Boswell, p. 47.

largest corporation of all – the universe. Finally, Darwin's work, his many works, also preserved his good mental health. What is interesting is that, even though he did not suffer severely from it (his stutter, in fact, was a symptom of the despairing nervousness I believe), he knew what his work was saving him from and, possibly, this was one reason why he worked so hard. Toward the end of his life, Darwin's son Robert, Charles Darwin's father, urged him to work less hard at his medical practice. Darwin replied:

It is a dangerous experiment, and generally ends either in drunkenness or hypo-chondriacism. Thus I reason, one must do something (so country squires fox-hunt), otherwise one grows weary of life, and becomes prey to ennui. There-fore one may as well do something advantageous to oneself and friends or to mankind, as employ oneself in cards or other things equally insignificant.[42]

I have searched through Darwin's fascinating medical treatise, the *Zoonomia*, for his description of something like the disease of the learned. But even though Darwin is often mentioned by medical his-torians as important in the history of the treatment of mental illness, he does not seem to discuss Hume's disease of the learned as such. He does discuss what he calls *Taedium vitae*, or the "irksomeness of life," but this is primarily a disease of middle-aged people in Darwin's treatise:

Taedium vitae. The inanity of sublunary things has afforded a theme to philoso-phers, moralists, divines, from the earliest records of antiquity; "Vanity of vani-ties!" says the preacher, "all is vanity!" Nor is there any one, I suppose, who has passed the meridian of life, who has not at some moments felt the nihility of all things.[43]

Part of the treatment for the problem is activity, work, suggestive of Darwin's rejoinder on retirement: "The cultivation of science, as of chemistry, natural philosophy, natural history, which supplies an inex-haustible source of pleasurable novelty, and relieves ennui by the ex-ertions it occasions." [44] Darwin's whole coverage of the symptoms of and treatments for ennui and melancholy suggests his defensive positivism. If one does not work in the step by step Lockean manner, there is apt to be decline. In fact, the rigors of hard work constitute the best defense against nervousness and despair.

The letters of Thomas Gray indicate that he often busied himself with making lists – records of the temperature, lists of plant growth, anti-

---

[42] Pearson, p. 219.
[43] Darwin, *Zoonomia*, Second Part, First American Edition (Philadelphia: Dobson, 1797), I, 468.
[44] *Ibid.*, p. 471.

quarian catalogues – in order to relieve depression. Typical is the following from a letter of 1758:

> The drift of my present studies is to know, wherever I am, what lies within reach [monuments, buildings] that may be worth seeing; whether it be building, ruin, park, garden, prospect, picture, or monument. To whom it does, or has belonged, and what has been the characteristic and taste of different ages. You will say, this is the object of all antiquaries. But pray, what antiquary ever saw these objects in the same light, or desired to know them for a like reason? In short, say what you please, I am persuaded whenever my list is finished, you will approve it, and think it of no small use. My spirits are very near the *freezing-point*; and for some hours of the day, this exercise, by its warmth and gentle motion, serves to raise them a few degrees higher.[45]

Although Johnson and Gray have very little good to say of each other, they agree in their dislike of Hume. (Significantly enough, the two writers closest to the London literary scene seem to harbor the most violent dislikes of each other and of the other two although the only connection I can see between Gray and Darwin – other than in the mood of despair, of course – is that Darwin was an undergraduate at Cambridge about the time Gray's unhappiness with the undergraduates in Peterhouse forced him to change colleges.) Gray's objection to Hume is that his skepticism encourages almost random attention to minute details, and hence it is valueless. But this pursuit of one's personal inclinations as they crop up is very similar to the pursuit of "sentiment" or personal "sensibility" – even to the making of lists. Gray writes with tension and even a touch of self-disgust about Hume because what he describes he has done continually himself:

> ...I have always thought David Hume a pernicious writer, and believe he has done as much mischief here as he has in his own country. A turbid and shallow stream often appears to our apprehensions very deep. A professed skeptic can be guided by nothing but his present passions (if he has any) and interests; and to be masters of his philosophy we need not his books or advice, for every child is capable of the same thing, without any study at all.[46]

In a very recent essay, Jean Hagstrum argues that Gray was continually making things, large or small, as they interested him – from journies to lists to poems – in order to conceal and to control a persistent melancholy. Hagstrum labels both the problem and the solution "sensibility." I heard the essay read at a conference on Gray which I attended while working out my own ideas on "comic materialism," and Hagstrum's

[45] To Dr. Wharton, February 21, 1758. In Gray, p. 207.
[46] To Mr. Beattie, July 2, 1770. *Ibid.*, p. 312.

ideas rang true to what I had discovered and thought. The paper is called "Gray's Sensibility," and Hagstrum writes:

Gray might have joined his beloved dead by an unnatural act had it not been for his intellectual and artistic interests – the notebook jottings as well as the letters, the bibliographical lists as well as the poetic lines. It is precisely because *sensibility* is a term broad enough to include all these interests and dispositions that I have preferred it as a title to *melancholy*, even though melancholy is the more basic and potent word.[47]

The thing that immediately strikes us in this term "sensibility" and then in the mood and type of literature that it designates is its deceptive circling or doubling around upon itself. The term refers to, insofar as it means random sentiments or interests, the extreme despair, almost desperation, of a valueless system. But the term also carries a highly optimistic connotation. It means a complete and cheerful acceptance of this valueless system and a solution to it by attention to the novelty and empirical reality of separate and unique sentiments. Sensibility is the emotional and artistic equivalent of Lockean epistemology or Newton's "mathematical way," and like its two philosophic cousins it both hides and is motivated by the abyss of valuelessness. Like the calculus, individual sentiments and interests may approach fixed truth, but if they were ever to reach it they would lose their validity as individual sentiments.

Northrop Frye's pioneering essay on this literature of uncertainty entitled "Towards Defining an Age of Sensibility" speaks of a poetry of process rather than product, which, in a sense, is a license for a proliferating modern literature of incomplete, tentative lists.[48] What devastating support for Bate's analysis that modern writers somehow know, and are frustrated by the fact that they cannot do the complete, final things earlier writers did! A poetry of process means a Lockean poetry of accumulating points of data – emotional data. Its emphasis on novelty and intense and varying sentiment belies and hides the familiar despair

[47] Jean Hagstrum, "Gray's Sensibility" read at the conference on *Gray and the Humanist Tradition* held at Carleton University, Ottawa, Canada, May 17-20, 1971. Professor Hagstrum has kindly given me a copy of the manuscript of his essay which is due to be published soon by Carleton University as part of a volume of essays on Gray from the 1971 conference.

[48] Northrop Frye, "Towards Defining an Age of Sensibility," in *ELH, A Journal of English Literary History*, 23. (June, 1956). The critical literature about this "age" is growing. See in particular the special issue of *Eighteenth-Century Studies* devoted to it. 4, no. 1 (Fall, 1970) as well as the volume of essays *From Sensibility to Romanticism* edited by Frederick W. Hilles and Harold Bloom (New York: Oxford Univ. Press, 1965).

we have seen – the despair of having points on the right and points on the left but nothing final and permanent in the middle.

In Darwin's case, it is better to label this sensibility "comic materialism" for two reasons. First of all, his use of sentiment in poetry has a strongly consistent materialistic rationale behind it, which is interesting and instructive for the general study of literature because of its extreme nature. I will describe this almost anti-literary, Lockean aesthetic in the next two chapters. We can recall Locke's suspicion and dislike of the role of the poet. Darwin's analysis leads him to a similar suspicion; but Darwin, of course, also is a poet. And here is the second reason for the appropriateness of the term "comic materialism." Comic irony is indispensable for Darwin in the fact of the uncertainties and self-contradictions that his skeptical analytic thought reveals.

Here again the abject despair implicit in the half-knowledge of Darwin's materialism, if it is taken seriously, reminds me of Johnson and of Gray. But the comic, almost carefree, defense against the puzzles of the infinite universe reminds me of the puckish Hume as he is described by a recent critic in the guise of his ideal skeptic:

Such a skeptic will be modest, diffident, and careless. He will come to some degree of doubt, and will always see the lack of rational basis for any conclusion. He will, sometimes, realize that he reasons in the careless manner of speculating owing to an inclination of the moment, of accepting a conclusion *pro tem.* because of the way it strikes him, etc.[49]

Darwin was a free-wheeling analyst and theorist with a highly developed sense of irony.[50] Some of his theories and writings are worth more attention – even if only because they are amusing. The editor of the only recent anthology of Darwin's writings says, "... it was the Lunar [Darwinian] tradition to be light-hearted at every opportunity." [51]

---

[49] Richard H. Popkin, "David Hume: His Pyrrhonism and His Critique of Pyrrhonism," in *Hume*, V. C. Chappell, ed., (Notre Dame: University of Notre Dame Press, 1968), p. 96.

[50] Darwin speculated that the language needed a new mark of punctuation to indicate irony. He proposed an inverted question-mark. See "Additional Notes" to *The Temple of Nature* (1803).

[51] Desmong King-Hele, ed., *The Essential Writings of Erasmus Darwin* (London: MacGibbon & Kee, 1968), p. 38.

CHAPTER TWO

DARWIN'S LITERARY THEORY

> Hence the reverberations in the words
> Of his first central hymns, the celebrants
> Of rankest trivia, tests of the strength
> Of his aesthetic, his philosophy.
>
> Wallace Stevens,
> "The Comedian as the Letter C"

I

A serious, pious view of literature (that is the general concept of verbal human art) as eternally the same obsessed and inhibited many writers of the 18th century. The authoritarian example of the "ancients" was indeed one of the "ghosts" of innate verities that Lockean analysis could not dismiss. Darwin himself could not help but pay devote homage to the general ideas about the mimetic power of literature to hold the mirror up to truth and nature. But Darwin had much more ability and inclination to speculate than, like Pope, to polish epigrammatic condensations of inherited traditions. Thus, even though the nervous tone of his writing seems in part forced out under the burden of the past, what is interesting about his literary theory is its daring speculation about the physiological explanation of literary art.

Theorizing, even playful speculation, was paradoxically consistent with the new analytic methodology. It was also a corollary of the univocal world view that said that all phenomena was made of the same material in different arrangements. This univocal world view, of course, was the biggest theory of all; and here we are back at the indeterminacy of the Newtonian-Lockean method that is so maddeningly circular but which has proved so workable. In any case, theory, daring theory, along with step-by-step analysis is a characteristic of this method. Historians of science have shown that despite, or rather complimentary to, his coy disclaimer, *Hypotheses non fingo*, Newton was a daring theorizer who taught the best of the scientists that followed him to try to discover new connections between things by speculating.[1] Darwin begins both of his

---

[1] See in particular: I. Bernard Cohen, *Franklin and Newton* (Philadelphia: American Philosophical Society, 1956), but also a new biography of Einstein

two major works of the 90s, the complete *Botanic Garden,* a poem, and the prose *Zoonomia* with nervous assurances that, in spite of pious tradition and empiricism, he will speculate boldly:

> It may be proper here to apologize for many of the subsequent conjectures on some articles of natural philosophy, as not being supported by accurate investigation or conclusive experiments. Extravagant theories, however, in those parts of philosophy where our knowledge is yet imperfect, are not without their use; as they encourage the execution of laborious experiments, or the investigation of ingenious deductions, to confirm or refute them. And, since natural objects are allied to each other by many affinities, every kind of theoretic distribution of them adds to our knowledge by developing some of their analogies.
>
> . . . .
>
> The purport of the following pages is an endeavour to reduce the facts belonging to *Animal Life* in classes ... to unravel the theory of diseases.... The want of a theory, deduced from such strict analogy, to conduct the practice of medicine, is lamented by its professors.... There are some modern practicioners who declaim against medical theory in general, not considering that to think is to theorize; and that no one can direct a method of cure to a person labouring under disease without thinking, that is, without theorizing; and happy therefore is the patient, whose physician possesses the best theory.[2]

Newton had hinted at a unified theory of physical motion in his concept of the "aether." Others, including Franklin, were beginning to imagine a unified theory of electrical motion. But Darwin, the medical man, says here that he wants a unified theory of "animal" motion, of life. Like countless other natural philosophers, and *philosophes* in France, Darwin never quite synthesizes a totally workable theory of life processes at any given time or over time; but he did put together primitive versions of what have now become our modern theories of electro-chemical physiology and of biological evolution. Also, Darwin's desire for a unified theory for medicine recalls earlier doctors and physiologists of the 18th century who sought a unified theory of body and matter, who wanted to do for life studies what Newton had done for physics. We assume that Darwin read and assimilated the work of the physiologists Boerhaave and Haller and of David Hartley, the English associationist, because they are cited in the *Zoonomia*. Boerhaave in particular, like Darwin, ex-

---

makes the same point about theory in science. See Ronald W. Clark, *Einstein: The Life and Times* (New York: World, 1970). "[Einstein] retained a touch of clowning humour as well as a resigned and understanding amusement at the follies of the human race," p. 3.

[2] Erasmus Darwin, *The Botanic Garden, A Poem, in Two Parts,* The Second American Edition, (New York: T. & J. Swords, 1807), xxii. and *Zoonomia; or The Laws of Organic Life,* First American Edition (New York: T. & J. Swords, 1796), pp. 1-2.

pressly stated his desire to discover a life theory that would unite medical knowledge.[3]

What we do not know is how familiar Darwin was with the writings of Boerhaave's notorious student, La Mettrie, the author of *L'Homme machine* (1748) who absorbed the brunt of the attack against "atheistic materialists" in the second half of the century. Even though Darwin makes no mention of him, we can assume that he must have known La Mettrie's work because he rather inherited the notoriety, among English readers at least, for being a materialist of the extreme La Mettrie type.[4] Perhaps Darwin, in fact, carefully avoids mentioning La Mettrie as part of his prudent equivocation about commitment one way or another to religion. Irwin Primer, in an important article on Darwin, calls this the "double truth" strategy that radical thinkers of the time, especially in France, had to adopt.[5] In any case, La Mettrie had proposed the most radical life theory of all: that matter is fully capable of producing by itself all the phenomena we associate with life. And Darwin's notions on physiology seem much closer to that kind of desire for a univocal theory than to the Deistic, and hence dualistic, theories of the other physiologists such as Hartley. For example, at least half of Hartley's *Observations on Man* (1749) is devoted to a discussion of how associationist psychology supports theology. Darwin writes on the association of ideas and on other psychological and physiological matters, but never on theology.

Although we cannot possibly discuss all of the sources of Darwin's ideas, I should make one further observation to suggest that Darwin knew La Mettrie's work. As we shall see, one of the basic characteristics of living matter, according to Darwin, is irritative motion or "irritability," and although this notion has a long history in the 17th and 18th centuries La Mettrie seems to have made one of the firmest uses of it. In the Newtonian-Lockean tradition of trying to strip down to and uncover the dynamics of the ultimate particles, "La Mettrie . . . views the phenomenon of irritability as the key to the mystery of life itself, and proposes to erect the mechanistic theory of mind on this firm biological foundation." [6] What La Mettrie concluded, then, was the most daring, univocal speculation of all: "Let us then conclude boldly that man is a

[3] Aram Vartanian, *La Mettrie's L'Homme machine, A Study in the Origins of an Idea* (Princeton: Princeton U. Press, 1960), pp. 76-77.

[4] Hesketh Pearson, *Doctor Darwin* (New York: Walker and Company, 1963), pp. 138-144.

[5] Irwin Primer, "Erasmus Darwin's *Temple of Nature*: Progress, Evolution, and Eleusinian Mysteries," in *JHI*, 25 (Jan.-March, 1964), 58-76.

[6] Vartanian, p. 22.

machine, and that in the whole universe there is but a single substance differently modified. ..." [7] This dynamics would encompass everything – including literature. And so if we are to understand Darwin's views about the nature and role of literature, we must first look at his theory about the physiology of mental phenomena.

II

An earlier student of Darwin's overall accomplishment puts it well:

He believes that all appetites and all intellectual life can be explained on the basis of physiology. Analyze organic life with its muscles, nerves, and fibres, and you will discover the source of not only the physical, but also the intricate moral and emotional life of mankind. It is a theory which fascinated the psychologists, and which, as presented by David Hartley, stamped its mark – for a time, at least – on the new generation of poets, Coleridge and Wordsworth. It was out of this system of aestho-physiology that Erasmus Darwin's theory of poetry and fine art grew.[8]

Similarly, when Jean Hagstrum writes on Samuel Johnson's literary criticism, he begins by explaining Johnson's notions of mind. But for Johnson it has to be a psychology of mind in which unobservable general faculties are invoked. He does not believe in the possibility of a univocal physiology of mind. In fact, as we know, Johnson was stubbornly dualistic in spite of, or perhaps because of, his allegiance to experience: "Johnson vigorously opposed the *école sensualiste*. . . . For Johnson the mind is as completely spiritual as matter is completely 'inert, senseless, and lifeless.' " [9]

Whereas Johnson accepts the unexplainable and essentially unobservable dichotomy between spirit and matter, Darwin is characteristic of the intellectual effort to resolve the dualism that has confused western man since Newton's time. As Father Boyd says, the beginning assumption is univocal – the assumption that there must be a uniformity among all things, and that it is probably material. A primary problem has continually been that, even though all things may be made of matter, it is difficult to explain motion. Darwin is typical of many attempting a univocal explanation as he squirms around trying to theorize about matter in motion. The way he begins is deceptive because he states the

[7] La Mettrie, *Man a Machine* in Lester G. Crocker, ed., *The Age of Enlightenment* (New York: Harper & Row, 1969), p. 103.

[8] James V. Logan, *The Poetry and Aesthetics of Erasmus Darwin* (Princeton: Princeton Univ. Press, 1936), p. 21. Logan, who has done the most scholarly work on Darwin, is a little sketchy on the psychology, but very good on the aesthetics.

[9] Jean H. Hagstrum, *Samuel Johnson's Literary Criticism* (Chicago: Univ. of Chicago Press, 1952), p. 8.

dualism as though it had no resolution. He generalizes, early in the *Zoonomia*, that the "whole of nature" consists of two "essences or substances": spirit and matter. "The former of these possesses the power to commence or produce motion, and the latter to receive and communicate it." [10]

He goes on to theorize, then, that the motions of matter are of three kinds, and we assume at this point that they each must be initiated by spirit. The three kinds of motion, according to Darwin, are gravitational motion, chemical motion, and animal motion. We assume that the first kind of motion is initiated by the "spirit of gravitation" – what Newton and Franklin theorized about as the "aether." It would seem that what is significant about Newton's theorizing about the "aether" is that he wanted to find a physical explanation for motion, and not just let it be as "spirit." The second, chemical motion, Darwin admits has not been studied much. The third kind of motion, which in Darwin's observation is really the phenomenon of irritability [he usually calls it contraction] in living tissue, is initiated by the "spirit of animation." He is very careful to distinguish this kind of motion from the other two, gravity and chemistry, because he knows that he cannot explain the "twitching" motion of living tissue by either of these, and he wants explanations – not just ghostlike spirits:

Hence, when we say animal motion is excited by irritation, we do not mean that the motion bears any proportion to the mechanical impulse of the stimulus; nor that it is affected by the general gravitation of the two bodies; nor by their chemical properties, but solely that certain animal fibres are excited into action by something external to the moving organ.[11]

As his explanation continues, however, it becomes clear that he is working very hard to explain the impossible – the vanishing point where reaction of matter becomes initiated action, where the ultimate particles "cause" matter to move. Darwin gets no farther than any of the other theorizers did; but the significant fact is that he is trying for a physical explanation, assuming that there is one. The resulting indeterminacy is both amusing and brave:

For nothing can act, where it does not exist; for to act includes to exist; and therefore the particles of the muscular fibre (which in its state of relaxation are supposed not to touch) cannot affect each other without the influence of some intermediate agent; this agent is here termed the spirit of animation, or sensorial power, but may with equal propriety be termed the power, which causes con-

[10] Darwin, *Zoonomia*, p. 3.
[11] *Ibid.*, p. 10.
[12] *Ibid.*, p. 44.

traction; or may be called by any other name, which the reader may choose to affix to it.[12]

Even though Darwin cannot explain exactly how, the spirit of animation for him is finally material – not immaterial at all. It is like Newton's "aether" or Franklin's elastic stuff. It somehow shares properties with matter because otherwise how could it affect matter at all, and hence it is material:

No two things can influence or affect each other, which have not some property common to both of them.... Hence the spirit of animation, at the time it communicates or receives motion from solid bodies, must itself possess some property of solidity. And in consequence at the time it receives other kinds of motion from light, it must possess that property, which light possesses, to communicate that kind of motion; and for which language has no name, unless it be termed Visibility. And at the same time it is stimulated into other kinds of animal motion by the particles of sapid and odorous bodies affecting the senses of taste and smell, it must resemble these particles of flavour, and of odour, in possessing some similar or correspondent property....[13]

Thus Darwin's physiology and psychology are grounded in a univocal matter theory. Spirit becomes no different from matter. At least there is "some property common to both of them."

Once he has explained how motion gets into the nervous system of the body, what he calls the "sensorium," the rest of the linkages from sense perception to all mental and physical activity are explained by a system of mechanical imitation and association of ideas. Ideas themselves are simply repetitions in nerve fibres of original "irritations" on sense organs, and, as Hartley had explained, they are built up of "aggregates" of many of these repetitions. Complex ideas, then, are constructed from original sense "irritations" on the principle of the association of ideas. The key source of "irritation," and hence of knowledge about the external world, is the sense of touch. The other senses, sight in particular, are like invisible translations of touch. The key here is that Darwin considers motion to be synonymous with a change in figure or shape, and so the way to "read" motion is through touch. He writes, "... *motion may be defined to be a variation of figure*; for the whole universe may be considered as one thing possessing a certain figure; the motions of any of its parts are a variation of this figure of the whole...." [14]

Once animal motion begins, for Darwin, it is retained and passed on by its translation from one to the other of four kinds of animal motion that he theorizes exist in the human sensorium. These four kinds of

[13] *Ibid.*, pp. 81-82. The italics are Darwin's.
[14] *Ibid.*, p. 10. The italics are Darwin's.

motion are, in the order of increasing conscious control: 1) irritative
motion (sense perception) 2) sensitive motion (involuntary responses –
dreams, etc.) 3) associative motion 4) voluntary motion (reason, etc.).
In this way, memory and the different varieties of thinking are a continual reshuffling of animal motion. And there is no other source of
knowledge than from original irritative motion and from the continual
recombinations of this in the sensorium. For Darwin, the mystery of
mental phenomena is simply the mystery of intricate networks of association and perception.[15] These need to be steadily mapped in order to
understand the human mind. But, unlike the motions of gravity, there
is little assurance that animal motions will always follow similar patterns.
In fact, experience tells us that these motions tend to produce a variety
of new effects more readily, for instance, than gravity does. Given its
accumulative nature, it would seem that there can be no general, valid
map for the possibilities of animal motion.

III

To give some idea of the potential for uncertainty and relativism with
regard to artistic taste inherent in such a physiology of perception, we
can turn to David Hume again for a moment. Hume was uncanny about
pushing the implications of analysis and the Lockean assumptions about
perception to their extremes, and Darwin's physiology and psychology
are simply elaborations of the Lockean assumptions. In his essay "Of
the Standard of Taste," Hume says that literary taste is no different from
the taste for food in man – purely physical, extremely varied, and whimsi-
cally different according to individuals. He writes playfully, "To seek
the real beauty, or real deformity, is as fruitless an enquiry, as to pretend
to ascertain the real sweet or real bitter. According to the disposition of
the organs, the same object may be both sweet and bitter; and the
proverb has justly determined it to be fruitless to dispute concerning

---

[15] Darwin often versifies his theories; and even though, as we shall see, verse
constitutes the "looser analogies" a few lines from *The Temple of Nature* (1803)
illustrate well his notion of the accumulation of mental phenomena from perception:

> Give to my ear the progress of the Mind.
> How loves, and tastes, and sympathies commence
> From evanescent notices of sense?
> How from the yielding touch and rolling eyes
> The piles immense of human science rise?
>
> Canto III, 11. 42-46.

[16] David Hume, "Of the Standard of Taste," in Ralph Cohen, ed., *Essential
Works of David Hume* (New York: Bantam Books, 1965), p. 451.

tastes." [16] Although he recognizes that taste can only be a welter of particular sensations, Hume does believe that eventually a consensus of the tastes of the "best" men will prevail and help control what is "tasted." Hume can be devilish and shocking because he believes that we can trust nature.

Darwin, also, is finally somewhat withdrawn and ironic, I believe, in the face of the fecund particularity of nature. But he does analyze what he can, and his physiology of animal motions gives him a kind of crude calculus for plotting the points of intersection at which "ideas" might produce literary pleasure. He will not accept a general term like "Beauty" without analyzing it. When he does analyze it, it ceases to exist as an independent quality and becomes the name for whatever produces pleasure in us.[17] Then, it becomes a question of analyzing pleasure, of finding or describing the combinations of animal motions, to continue to use his terms, that produce various kinds of pleasure. From the outset, he insists that the artificial products of culture can produce more pleasure than simple sense perception because there can be a variety of different kinds of animal motion involved whereas in simple sense perception only "irritative motion" is involved. In other words, in the calculus of pleasure man can experience higher level results because he is an intellectual being that has evolved other animal motions than those necessary for sense perception. This is a particular value in Darwin's physiological theorizing. It recalls Hartley's notion of ever accumulating vibrations leading eventually to God, and it tells us why we are men. We have developed more nervous machinery.

One source of additional pleasure than simple sense perception that Darwin explains well is the pleasure we receive from the added mental exercise necessary to observe repetitions. As well as explaining the mechanism for this pleasure we receive from observing repetition, Darwin also explains the point at which the returns begin to diminish and it ceases to be pleasure. In other words, the calculus of pleasure measures an equilibrium in which pleasure results from a certain level of activity that presumably could be measured. The following paragraph on repetition is one of his best applications of his physiology. What he calls "intuitive analogy" here results from a combination of what he calls voluntary motion and irritative motion. Voluntary motion, in turn, is the class of animal motion that includes reason, but in this case it is

[17] See his section on "Sentiment of Beauty" in Additional Note XIII, "Analysis of Taste," in *The Temple of Nature; a Poem* (New York: T. & J. Sword, 1804). I am using these later American editions of Darwin's works because I have them conveniently at home.

unconscious voluntary motion. One final definition to understand the paragraph: the "ideas of imagination" are involuntary animal motions or what he calls motions of sensation. They are stimulated by pleasure or pain "involuntarily." More on his notion of imagination later. Now his description of the particular level of pleasure from observing repetition. The pleasure comes from the circuitry of animal motion. Too much circuitry over-rides pleasure:

In our waking hours, a perpetual voluntary exertion, of which we are unconscious, attends all our new trains of ideas, whether those of imagination or of perception; which, by comparing them with our former experience, preserves the consistency of the former, by rejecting such as are incongruous; and adds to the credibility of the latter, by their analogy to objects of our previous knowledge: and this exertion is attended with pleasurable sensation. After very frequent repetition, these trains of ideas do not excite the exertion of this intuitive analogy, and, in consequence, are not attended with additional pleasure to that simply of perception; and, by continued repetition, they at length lose even the pleasure simply of perception, and thence finally cease to be excited: whence one cause of the torpor of old age, and of death. . . .[18]

It should be clear that in Darwin's conception of this particular kind of pleasure, at least, there is nothing constant. The pleasure results from a certain combination of motion, and presumably it could change as the organism changes. Darwin also isolates and describes other combinations or animal motions that produce pleasure. Not many of these situations that Darwin describes were first noticed by him. He reworks ideas common all during the century among writers on aesthetics of what might be called the empirical school of Locke who were trying to analyze the sources of literary pleasure. His pinpointing of repetition, for instance, and of novelty, which he discusses earlier, owes something to the continuing discussion of "uniformity amidst variety." [19] What is interesting and new in Darwin's treatment is the sense of close measurement, of plotting the direction of two or more kinds of animal motion until they intersect and we get added pleasure from the additional mental activity.

Taste, or pleasure from the productions of culture, can be improved or increased by exercise or practice, according to Darwin. We would expect this to be the case in his analysis since what he is describing seems to be essentially a quantitative phenomenon:

[18] *Ibid.,* p. 219.
[19] The phrase "uniformity amidst variety" is from Francis Hutcheson, *An Inquiry into the Original of our Ideas of Beauty and Virtue* (1725). See Logan for a good account of these relations between Darwin's aesthetics and the aesthetics of the school of Locke, pp. 46-92.

It should here be observed, that as the pleasure of novelty is produced by the exertion of our voluntary power in comparing uncommon objects with those which are more usually exhibited, this sentiment of novelty is less perceived by those who do not readily use the faculty of volition, or who have previous knowledge of nature, as by very ignorant or very stupid people, or by brute animals; and that, therefore, to be affected with this circumstance of the objects of Taste requires some previous knowledge of such kinds of objects, and some degree of mental exertion.[20]

One of the only qualitative considerations in Darwin's whole discussion of the potentiality for pleasure that exists in our intricate systems of animal motion is treated under the heading "Association of agreeable Sentiments with visible Objects" in his long note on taste. The pleasures of association can be quantitative, of course – more mental exercise regardless of what is associated, elephants or peachtrees. But one constant in human association seems to be sexual perception, in particular, the curving shape of the female bosom. In fact, for Darwin a good bit of the pleasure necessary to designate something "beautiful" derives from the associations with the perception (and remembered perception) of the female shape. Interestingly and modernly enough, he grounds our interest in the female shape in early childhood experience. We will consider this in some detail in the next chapter on visualism, but it is appropriate here to end this discussion of taste with a quotation from Darwin on at least one source of pleasure that seems to be constant: "The sentiment of Beauty appears to be attached from our cradles to the easy curvatures of lines, and smooth surfaces of visible objects, and to have been derived from the form of the female bosom." [21]

IV

If the physiology of taste is going to be convincing, there must be some explanation of the mysterious powers of matter in animal motion to create strange, hallucinatory ideas that is more than just a quantitative explanation. There must be some locating of the mental powers of imagination. The creative imagination cannot be just simple sense perception because we know what mankind has created with this faculty. In a sense, no physiology, least of all the beginnings in the 18th century, has succeeded in locating and describing the mysteries of the imagination. One recent scholar is very hard indeed on the 18th-century materialists-physiologists, and he says that their failure to explain the

---

[20] Darwin, *Temple of Nature*, p. 216.
[21] *Ibid.*, p. 224.

imagination opened the gates for the myth theorizers of the Romantic era down to our own day:

Enlightenment scientists, try though they did, were unable to explain adequately the interaction of the imagination and the animal spirits. If they had tackled a less important matter, they might have been forgiven, but theirs was the single most important problem of physiology.... Some aspects of their failure were overlooked because culture, particularly in England, was prepared to accept these failures. The inability of the neurologist, for example, to devise a calculus for this interaction was viewed less disappointedly because society at large had not as yet become quantified in the sense we have known technological quantification in this century.[22]

Darwin, of course, is part of this failure, and this is one explanation why his ideas have lain dormant so long during the growth of myth explanations of imagination. But Darwin did not fail quite as severely as the strict scientists referred to above because Darwin did not restrict himself just to quantifying animal motion. He theorized far beyond his ability to quantify, which, of course, to us is a sign of failure; but at the same time he rejected all explanations that were not physical. Thus he describes operations of animal motion, of the mind, that only now we are beginning to isolate and to measure – such as the function and power of dreams and the unconscious or the "involuntary" operation of the imagination. Actually, the materialists discovered the real existence of the imagination, the intricate circuitry of the mind; and La Mettrie was one of the first to praise the unconscious powers of animal motion as the only source of knowledge we have.[23] It was just that they could not supply all that they promised. They could not quantify the mysterious.

Darwin is pretty good in his theorizing about what he classifies as the involuntary sensitive motions. They are extremely powerful because they are inbred and self-contained, so to speak. When he describes the "catenations" or linkages [circuitry] of voluntary motions, such as recollection or the attempted control of stuttering, for instance, they have strange, wide-ranging possibilities.[24] Thus, his other category of involuntary motion has the potential for even stranger catenation. It is in the latter category that he places imagination as one of the motions of sensation. And since sensation [this should be distinguished from perception in Darwin's terminology] has nothing to do but concern itself with itself the mental power generated may be strong and mysterious:

[22] G. S. Rousseau, "Science and the Discovery of the Imagination in Enlightened England," in *Eighteenth-Century Studies*, 3, (Fall, 1969), 127.
[23] See Vartanian, pp. 28 ff.
[24] See Darwin, *Zoonomia*, pp. 139-142.

There is a criterion by which we may distinguish our voluntary acts or thoughts from those that are excited by our sensations. The former are always employed about the *means* to acquire pleasurable objects, or to avoid painful ones: while the latter are employed about the *possession* of those that are already in our power.25

One advantage of this theory is that it allows Darwin to explain the power of dreams. In sleep none of our voluntary motions operate, and so the ideas in our dreams result from the involuntary motions of sensation given free rein. His explanation makes it clear that, if we do not dream, we will become sick because the involuntary motions will overflow into waking life and force out the voluntary motions of reason, memory, etc. His theory sounds very modern at this point, and certainly not a failure to suggest complexity:

This perpetual flow of the trains of ideas which constitute our dreams, and which are caused by painful or pleasureable sensations, might, at first view, be conceived to be an useless expenditure of sensorial power. But it has been shown that those motions which are perpetually excited, as those of the arterial system by the stimulus of the blood, are attended by a great accumulation of sensorial power, after they have been for a time suspended; as the hot-fit of fever is the consequence of the cold one. Now, as these trains of ideas, caused by sensation, are perpetually excited during our waking hours, if they were to be suspended in sleep like the voluntary motions, (which are exerted only by intervals during our waking hours) an accumulation of sensorial power would follow; and on our awaking, a delirium would supervene; since these ideas, caused by sensation, would be produced with such energy, that we should mistake the trains of imagination for ideas excited by irritation.26

It seems clear that for Darwin the equilibrium of motions in the mind is not at all simple, and there seems to be great potential for creative or unusual combinations. In fact, voluntary motions such as reason occur much less frequently than sensitive, imaginative motions. Even though his theoretical physiology, along with that of other materialists, has not gotten a good press, one recent scholar of the Romantic movement credits Darwin with coming as close as any 18th-century theorist to an explanation of the imagination that was intricate enough to influence Coleridge. Elizabeth Schneider argues that Coleridge got a good bit of his notion of "dramatic illusion" or the "willing suspension of disbelief" from Darwin: "In his treatment of this whole subject Coleridge is much closer to Darwin than to any other predecessor that I know of." 27 What

25 *Ibid.*, p. 133. The italics are Darwin's.
26 *Ibid.*, p. 145.
27 Elizabeth Schneider, *Coleridge, Opium, and Kubla Khan* (Chicago: University of Chicago Press, 1953), p. 101.

she is referring to is Darwin's explanation of what happens when, under the influence of an art or possibly a disease, the involuntary motions of sensation take over the mind completely while we are awake. This is extreme imagination or "suspension of disbelief," and the mental phenomenon, although wild and mysterious, is perfectly understandable when it is compared to the mechanism of our dreams:

When, by the art of the Painter or Poet, a train of ideas is suggested to our imaginations, which interests us so much by the pain or pleasure it affords, that we cease to attend to the irritations of common external objects, and cease also to use any voluntary efforts to compare these interesting trains of ideas with our previous knowledge of things [intuitive analogy], a complete reverie is produced: during which time, however short, if it be but for a moment, the objects themselves appear to exist before us. This, I think has been called, by an ingenious critic, "the ideal presence" of such objects. (Elements of Criticism by Lord Kaimes [sic.]).[28]

Although Darwin is close to theorizing about what we now call the unconscious and although his explanation of the therapeutic value of dreams sounds very modern and his discussion of imagination much like Coleridge, he is no Romantic because he insists that all these mental traits are potentially measureable and that none of them can create anything new beyond the original input of irritative motion or sense perception. Perhaps there is something dangerous in such non-pious brashness, or rather what it tells us is that we are totally alone with our sense perceptions and recombinations of them. Darwin knew this and undoubtedly winced. Hence his comic tone. But nevertheless he could not theorize that our imaginings held anything beyond their original irritability: "So far are we governed by the catenations of motions, which affect both the body and the mind of man, and which begin with our irritability, and end with it." [29]

V

A problem for the artist is to find a way to induce and to control this imaginative state in his audience. Darwin had grown up and come to know poetry during the heyday of the mid-century aesthetic school of the Whartons and Gray who had carefully studied ways to induce the imaginative state. Gray's famous series of pronouncements on poetic

[28] Darwin, *The Botanic Garden,* Part Two, p. 43. Miss Schneider mentions Lord Kames and concludes that Darwin does a better job of explaining the phenomenon.
[29] Darwin, *Zoonomia,* p. 96.

diction indicate well the importance of a carefully premeditated style for these writers:

As to matter of style, I have this to say: The language of the age is never the language of poetry.... Our poetry ... has a language peculiar to itself; to which almost every one that has written has added something by enriching it with foreign idioms and derivatives; nay sometimes words of their own composition and invention.... Shakespeare's language is one of his principal beauties.... Every word in him is a picture.[30]

If, in Darwin's theorizing, imagination is neither irritative and hence reflective of the shape and figure of external objects nor is it controlled by voluntary motion that compares ideas to the shape of external objects, then it is indeed in a never-neverland of its own. And its language will be its own language. We may not be convinced that Darwin, nor Gray for that matter, have either one of them found the language of imagination; but at least they know that it is not the language of day to day voluntary motion.[31] The main characteristic of the latter is "strict" analogy, according to Darwin, a kind of continual, accurate comparison that for the sake of accuracy may tend to be abstract and almost two-dimensional. On the other hand, imaginative language is more flamboyant, more free-wheeling in its shuffling around of sense perception. It is almost as though the materialist-discoverers of the rich imaginative circuitry in the middle of the mind (somewhere between simple sense perception and reason) knew that this was where the power was, the vividness, but they had not figured out exactly what it was useful for. Actually, Darwin, and any deeply analytic materialist, knew that finally imagination could not be useful for anything because the self-centered, dramatic sense of importance which it conveyed was simply the coloring of the animal motion of our species (like the feathers of the peacock species) and not direct revelation of a universe that fit our species any more than it fit any other species.

But humans do have this level of animal motion that is useful for pleasure, and so the question for the artist is how to turn it on. Darwin sounds like Gray when he writes, in one of the light dialogue "Interludes" to "The Loves of the Plants":

[30] To Mr. West, April, 1741. Thomas Gray, *Gray's Poems Letters and Essays*, John Drinkwater and Lewis Gibbs, eds. (New York: Dutton, Everyman, 1912), pp. 136-37.
[31] Logan argues very strongly that Darwin is in favor of sensuous language for poetry, and hence not as artificial as he has been called. I disagree with Logan. Darwin does say that sensuous language is the language of imagination, but the language of imagination is more artificial than the everyday language of voluntary comparison, which can be abstract. See Logan, pp. 82-85.

Bookseller. It must require great art in the Painter or Poet to produce this kind
of deception.

Poet. The matter must be interesting from its sublimity, beauty, or novelty;
this is the scientific part; and the art consists in bringing these distinctly before
the eye, so as to produce (as above-mentioned) the ideal presence of the object,
in which the great Shakespeare particularly excels.

Bookseller. Then it is not of any consequence whether the representations correspond with nature?

Poet. Not if they so much interest the reader or spectator as to induce the
reverie above described. Nature may be seen in the market-place, or at the card-
table; but we expect something more than this in the playhouse or picture-room.[32]

Thus premeditated artificiality in the use of language ornament, especially language to produce visual effects, is necessary for the artist in order
to induce imaginative states. Darwin was somewhat of a student of
language (he was a student of everything) and especially of figures of
speech that produce imaginative effects. He observed accurately that the
English language was particularly suited to the making of personifications
which tended to increase the visualism of language: "And, in one respect, I believe the English language serves the purpose of poetry better
than the ancient ones; I mean in the greater ease of producing personifications; for. . . ." [33] We will consider the whole topic of visual effects in
the next chapter as it is the main characteristic of Darwin's artificiality.
His comment, however, on another figure of speech, simile, shows how
completely he believed in the need for artificiality in language in order
to induce the imaginative state:

Bookseller. Then a similie should not very accurately resemble the subject:

Poet. No; it would then become a philosophical analogy; it would be ratiocination instead of poetry: it need only so far resemble the subject, as poetry itself
ought to resemble nature.[34]

Darwin's physiology and psychology of inter-related levels of animal
motion in which there are no gaps and where the material substance in
motion, whatever it is, is homogeneous would allow for the possibility of
transference of sense data from one sense to another, what we now call
synesthesia. The homogeneity of matter has proved very useful in
modern electronics and even medicine where blind people are able "to
see" by means of touch, but for Darwin it also offered the possibility
(needless to say he was also fascinated by the mechanical and medical
possibilities) of another aesthetic tool for inducing imaginative states:

[32] Darwin, *The Botanic Garden*, Part Two, p. 44.
[33] *Ibid.*, p. 98.
[34] *Ibid.*, p. 65.

Sir Isaac Newton has observed, that the breadths of the seven primary colors in the Sun's image, refracted by a prism, are proportional to the seven musical notes of the gamut [scale], or to the intervals of the eight sounds contained in an octave, that is, proportional to the following numbers. . . . From this curious coincidence, it has been proposed to produce a luminous music, consisting of successions of combinations of colours, analogous to a tune in respect to the proportions above-mentioned. This might be performed by a strong light . . . passing through coloured glasses, and falling on a defined part of a wall, with moveable blinds before them, which might communicate with the keys of a harpsichord, and thus produce, at the same time, visible and audible music in unison with each other.35

The discovery of so much inter-relationship in matter and thus the possibility of transferring messages from one sense organ to another, in fact, the discovery of imagination itself is actually disheartening. Compared to his romantic followers, Darwin is very cautious in his celebration of the imagination because he knows that it does not lead anywhere except around and around within itself. In terms of the psychology of the sane man, Darwin believes that it is actually better for voluntary motions (intuitive analogy) to over-ride imagination most of the time in order to allow us to work with the strict analogies of accumulative reason. In fact, for Darwin it seems a sign of human weakness that the involuntary motions, even though he knows their power, are more active than the voluntary motions. In terms of the pleasures of the imagination, Darwin like Addison, at the beginning of the century, does not know quite what their usefulness is. In anticipation of the romantics, he is a little frightened of imagination because he knows more than Addison about how powerful the involuntary motions are. But, in sum, Darwin would like to harness the "looser analogies" in the service of a science that was leading toward deeper vision of man's lostness in the vast randomness of matter in motion. Aware of that vision and self-conscious about the loss of stature for humanity (and for literature) within it, Darwin's tone with regard to his poems is a little apologetic, puckishly defensive, and finally comic. The following "advertisement" to *The Botanic Garden* communicates well this tone:

The general design of the following sheets is to enlist Imagination under the banner of Science; and to lead her votaries from the looser analogies, which dress out the imagery of poetry, to the stricter ones, which form the ratiocination of philosophy. While their particular design is to induce the ingenious to cultivate the knowledge of Botany, by introducing them to the vestibule of that delightful science, and recommending to their attention the immortal works of the celebrated Swedish Naturalist Linnaeus.36

35 *Ibid.*, p. 97. Darwin did have a contract to invent a speaking machine, but he could not make one work very well. See Desmond King-Hele, ed., *The Essential Writings of Erasmus Darwin* (London: MacGibbon & Kee, 1968), p. 125 and p. 129.
36 Darwin, from "Advertisement" to *The Botanic Garden.*

CHAPTER THREE

THE PLAYFULNESS OF THE PICTURESQUE
THE MIRTH OF THE MATERIAL

the eye of Crispin, hung
On porpoises, instead of apricots,
And on silentious porpoises, whose snouts
Dibbled in waves that were mustachios,
Inscrutable hair in an inscrutable world.

Wallace Stevens,
"The Comedian as the Letter C"

I

Much is lost from literature when it is no longer thought to be divinely inspired nor concerned with permanent, spiritual values; but much remains also of vitality and vividness – the curve of beauty and even a base in sexuality. The physiology of artistic taste and the discovery of the imagination as a material function of the brain opened up literature to something akin to technological development, to progress. Darwin was one of many "engineers" of the imagination in the second half of the 18th century. He experimented with sensation and "imaginative motions," as he termed them, in order to build an art based on the theory that pleasure comes from the lively recombinations of sense perceptions at the near sub-conscious level of involuntary animal motion. In other words, he believed that pleasure could be engineered out of matter, that it did not spring whole from supernatural virtue. Wordsworth believed the same thing when he described "the very world, which is the world / Of all of us, – the place where, in the end, / We find our happiness, or not at all!" [1]

Critics have often noted that the gaudy, artificial art of the late 18th century that the Romantics reacted against was in fact a necessary and positive antecedent to Romanticism because it promoted the use of physical sense perception within the newly discovered matrix of the imagination. The Romantics simply spiritualized and idealized sense perception and the imagination whereas picturesque art, including the

---

[1] William Wordsworth, *The Prelude*, 1850 edition, Book XI, 11. 142-144.

playful vitality of Darwinian art, never went beyond a skeptical wariness of what it was playing with. "There is something engaging about Gilpin [one of the early "picturesque travelers" to cultivate sense perception for its own sake]: his anxiety that the study of picturesque beauty shall not be deemed unsuitable to the vocation of a clergyman. . . ." [2] Perhaps the uncertainty of Darwin's work with the imagination is the weakest element in his art, but it is also appealing because of its vitality, tentativeness, and variety. In fact, his theorizing about and experimentation with "imaginative motion" agrees completely with Christopher Hussey's interpretation of the historical role of late 18th-century art. I will quote Hussey's classic interpretation of the picturesque inserting Darwin's terminology in square brackets:

The picturesque phase through which each art passed, roughly between 1730 and 1830, was in each case a prelude to romanticism. It occurred at the point when an art shifted its appeal from the reason to the imagination. An art that addresses the reason [voluntary motions], even though it does so through the eye, does not stress visual qualities. The reason wants to know [intuitive analogy, memory, etc.] not to experience sensations [involuntary, imaginative motions]. The romantic movement was an awakening of sensation, and, among the other sensations, that of sight required exercising. Thus the picturesque interregnum between classic and romantic art was necessary in order to enable the imagination to form the habit of feeling through the eyes.[3]

Hussey goes on to draw the mainline Romantic conclusion that the highest art somehow spiritualizes the imaginative motions: "Picturesque art is imperfect art, but not necessarily bad art." [4]

Even Darwin's contemporaries, the contemporaries of the picturesque, yearned for the "perfect" art of high idealization (as we all do) and so they had to call his changing, momentary "pleasures" imperfect. Even Anna Seward, who is about as picturesque (that is, changing and various) and non-ideal a lady of fashion as the skeptical century could produce, knows that art should be permanent and elevating, not just entertaining:

---

[2] Elizabeth Manwaring, *Italian Landscape in Eighteenth Century England* (New York: Oxford U. Press, 1925), p. 184.

[3] Christopher Hussey, *The Picturesque, Studies in a Point of View,* With a New Preface by the Author (Hamden, Conn.: Archon Books, 1967), p. 4. The tendency of Romantics later on is to reject visualism all together as Coleridge does in chapter VI of the 1817 *Biographia Literaria*:

Under that despotism of the eye ... under this strong sensuous influence, we are restless because invisible things are not the objects of vision; and metaphysical systems, for the most part, become popular, not for their truth, but in proportion as they attribute to causes a susceptibility of being *seen,* if only our visual organs were sufficiently powerful. . . .

[4] *Ibid.,* p. 5.

Splendid and charming as is this poem [she is describing "The Loves of the Plants" before publication], yet, written upon the, I think, mistaken system, that nothing which is not imagery should find a place in poetry, the incessant profusion of ornament will perhaps be a disadvantage to the work in general. . . .[5]

Not just, nor even primarily the gaudy visualism (the experimental beginnings of modern technicolor and impressionism) makes the art of the picturesque interesting, but rather the precarious matter of tone. Recent students of literature seem very interested in the fragility and nervousness of tone in this period as evidenced by their desire to find names for it. This art of the picturesque is very similar, of course, to "sensibility" and the art of "comic materialism" mentioned earlier. In true Darwinian fashion, recent critics, including myself, will try different names and different theories to focus in on what is of interest to them. Martin Price, in the collection of essays entitled *From Sensibility to Romanticism*, refers to "The Picturesque Moment," and his title is significant because this is an art of momentary fulfillment with no promises of visionary insight. Such an art would have to be pugnacious and uncertain and continually moving. Such an art is not really art in the Greek-Platonic sense, but more like everyday, bustling animal activity. And such an art would necessarily be self-conscious, then, about its ordinariness and would try harder to excite "imaginative motions" through artificiality. Price's description is perfect for Darwin's playful pastiche of visualism and assertiveness that infuriated Wordsworth, but that must have made him look deeper into this world:

The picturesque moment is that phase of speculation – a recurrent one, as I have tried to indicate – where the aesthetic categories are self-sufficient. . . . sense of play is a conspicuous feature of later eighteenth-century sensibility. It takes the form of play-acting, of the pleasures in ruins and follies, of subtly contrived garden views designed to be seen in telling succession, of revivals of styles in literature and architecture, of exoticism, of that peculiar assertiveness that comes out of skepticism. . . . The skeptical mind, aware of the need for reasonable common truths but aware as well of the imaginative power of arbitrary structures and accidental associations, finds itself torn between external nature and the mind's art, between knowledge and power.[6]

---

[5] To William Hayley, 6 Oct. 1787. In *Letters of Anna Seward: Written Between the Years of 1784 and 1807*, Six Volumes (Edinburgh: Constable, and Co., 1811), I, p. 340.
[6] Martin Price, "The Picturesque Moment," in Frederick W. Hilles and Harold Bloom, eds., *From Sensibility to Romanticism* (New York: Oxford Univ. Press, 1965), pp. 262, 271.

II

Darwin was torn between a desire for human, permanent knowledge and the discovery of sources of power. This ambivalence accounts for his assertive, nervous tone. But, as part of the ambivalence, he worked hard to develop what he thought were the sources of imaginative motion – the sensual, the accidental, the varied. Since all animal motion derives from the irritative motions of touch and since, as he said, "the mute language of the touch is sight," the best way to stimulate the circuitry of involuntary imaginative motion and of associative motion is through words that evoke the sense of sight.[7] True visual qualities in objects do not mean any one thing. They are wide open to individual interpretation, to the stimulation of what Darwin called imaginative motions and associative motions, or individual associations of ideas. Visual qualities are unique, varied, and infinitely expressive. As compared to rational comparisons that are intended to mean definite things and that require voluntary attention, visual qualities in objects just *are*. The trend toward the picturesque in the 18th century was most simply a trend toward this chaos of texture, the aesthetic equivalent of empiricism. In fact, the study of aesthetics is the study of sources of pleasure separate from meaning. A Greek-Platonic art has no aesthetics separate from the deepest religious meanings. And in this early exploration of the chaos of aesthetic response, of taste, visual qualities were thought to be the key to stimulating imaginative motion. Darwin makes a clear statement of his principle of visualism for poetry in one of the "Interludes" to his first long poem:

... the principal part of the language of poetry consists of those words which are expressive of the ideas, which we originally receive by the organ of sight; and, in this, it nearly, indeed, resembles painting; which can express itself in no other way, but by exciting the ideas or sensations belonging to the sense of vision.[8]

The expressiveness and individual power of visual qualities began to appeal to literary men early in the century, and one of the best examples of the ambivalent appeal of visualism to a writer is in the gardening interests of Pope. Darwin worked with an expressive, uniquely visual garden later in the century; but it was Pope, as many scholars have noted, who early advocated the change from formal to landscape gardening in which expressive, visual qualities became more and more important.

---

[7] The quoted line is from *The Temple of Nature*, canto III, 1. 144.
[8] Erasmus Darwin, "The Loves of the Plants," part II of *The Botanic Garden,* Second American Edition (New York: T. & J. Swords, 1807), p. 91.

The difference is between a garden in which definite allegoric or emblematic figures or whole sections appear that have to be "read" and interpreted accurately and knowledgeably, and a garden in which there is little definite meaning but a plethora of visual textures – "a mighty maze," to chop off the first half of Pope's famous line about his garden from the beginning of *An Essay on Man*. The ambivalence, which is strong all through Pope's work and which becomes stronger for others later in the century as the solution becomes less easy, is that he wants the maze of visual, sensuous texture at the same time he wants a clearly "meant" order. In *Windsor-Forest*, he believes in this "Order in Variety" so firmly, but at the expense of genuine, chaotic visualism. Scholarship on Pope, however, is beginning to emphasize more his later acknowledgement of the complex personalness and uniqueness of the mind, his fascination with the chaos of the visual.[9] Pope's estate at Twickenham included allegoric and emblematic niches and statues, but his underground grotto was also uniquely individual and personal and visual. When he wrote about his estate and his grotto, he emphasized the public and "meaningful" allegory of his retreat because he believed in certain reasonable patterns for society; but ". . . the grotto, like the garden, had its private and natural turns: the variety of its rooms has not been sufficiently stressed, nor its essentially private iconography . . . expressive features, 'transitory images,' that irresistible occur only to the one man capable of grasping them." [10]

The reason that Pope did not stress the uniquely personal in his surroundings or in his life, even though these immediate qualities were what in part inspired him, was paradoxically that he knew in fact that this was where the imaginative power lay. And he knew that emphasized too much this power would lead to fecund dullness, to the nightmares of sleep, the chaos of half-lights that we call night, the insipid continual flow of sense perception and imaginative motion much like the continual gurgling of the natural spring in his grotto. These were all the chaotic things he hated so eloquently throughout the various editions of *The Dunciad*. In other words, Pope is the perfect early example of the dilemma which the picturesque would lead to and which Darwin's exuberant development of the imaginative motions of visualism illustrates.

Darwin's own garden, small like Pope's, but much more fecund,

[9] See in particular John Dixon Hunt, "Emblem and Expressionism in the Eighteenth-Century Landscape Garden," in *Eighteenth-Century Studies*, 4 (Spring, 1971), 294-317 and Maynard Mack, *The Garden and the City, Retirement and Politics in the Later Poetry of Pope, 1731-1743* (Toronto: Univ. of Toronto Press, 1969).

[10] Hunt, pp. 307-308.

various, and even watery may represent meaningless yet powerful con-
fusion. His garden was also technologically useful, a botanic garden like
many 18th-century doctors had to have to grow medicines, and this
illustrates the union of the concrete visual with the practical in a welter
of fecund motion. The truly aesthetic (that is, art divorced from moral
or philosophic meaning) and the truly technological are equally fluxing
and valueless. Whatever works is noted and used. Darwin describes his
garden in a note at the beginning of his poem entitled *The Botanic
Garden,* and in the note it seems decorous and contained – much like
Pope's grotto with its natural spring:

> The scenery is taken from a botanic garden about a mile from Lichfield, where a
> cold bath was erected by Sir John Floyer. There is a grotto surrounded by pro-
> jecting rocks, from the edges of which trickels a perpetual shower of water; and
> it is here represented as adapted to love-scenes, as being thence a proper residence
> for the modern goddess of Botany, and the easier to introduce the next poem on
> the Loves of the Plants. . . .[11]

The decorous little note helps to introduce the allegory of the poem
which is so fantastic and playful, so "imaginative," that we hardly notice
the fecundity of the garden itself. Anna Seward's description of Darwin's
development of the garden makes it seem much more fecund and various,
however, a true "symbol" for imaginative motion – more like Xanadu
than Twickenham:

> About the year 1777, Dr. Darwin purchased a little, wild, umbrageous valley, a
> mile from Lichfield, amongst the only rocks which neighbour that city to nearly.
> It was irriguous from various springs, and swampy from their plenitude. . . .
>
> One of its native features had long excited the attention of the curious; a rock,
> which, in the central depth of the glen, drops perpetually, about three times in a
> minute. Aquatic plants border its top and branch from its fissures. No length of
> summer drought abates, no rains increase its humidity, no frost congeals its
> droppings. The doctor cultivated this spot – "And Paradise was open'd in the
> wild."
>
> In some parts he widened the brook into small lakes, that mirrored the valley;
> in others, he taught it to wind between shrubby margins. Not only with trees of
> various growth did he adorn the borders of the fountain, the brook, and the
> lakes, but with various classes of plants, uniting the Linnaean science with the
> charm of landscape. . . .[12]

Another example of visualism and of the connection between the purely
aesthetic or picturesque and technology is the camera obscura. It is
both visual, of course, and also neutral in meaning like the expressive

[11] Darwin, *The Botanic Garden,* part I, p. 2.
[12] Quoted in Hesketh Pearson, *Doctor Darwin* (New York: Walker and Co.,
1963), pp. 157-58.

garden because the viewer points the "camera" and he can point it anywhere. One of the recent studies of Pope's visualism emphasizes this impressionistic implication of the camera obscura: "Pope himself acknowledges this crucial element of personal control over his mental activity . . . he explains that the varieties of image which the *camera obscura* recreates for him are invoked precisely 'when you have a mind to light it up.' " [13] One would think there would be definite "meaning" in the visual capturing, the exact mirroring, of objects; but actually all that is mirrored are the myriads of "secondary qualities." Then when these are reshuffled by the imaginative and associative motions there is an almost infinite possibility of recombination, but no final particles, no final meaning. And without the comparisons of voluntary motions there cannot even be the tentative "meaning" of reason. If we recall the skepticism described earlier, it is clear that the visual camera, although it conveys vividness and stimulates much imaginative motion, does not give meaning. It generates mental power, not knowledge. Photo albums and collages have no meaning by themselves.

The Lunar Society experimented with photography, and the son of Darwin's friend Wedgwood actually came close to developing a silver nitrate compound that would "fix" pictures. Tom Wedgwood's work undoubtedly was known to Darwin. It was done about the time of the publication of the two parts of *The Botanic Garden*, 1789-92.[14] Darwin characterized "The Loves of the Plants," part two but the first one published, as a camera obscura, choosing the perfect metaphor to indicate the random visualism, the roving camera eye technique, of his poetry. His introduction of the metaphor at the beginning of the 1789 volume sounds flip and assertive, another example of his nervous tone in the face of "meaningless" power:

Gentle Reader,
   Lo, here a Camera Obscura is presented to thy view, in which are lights and shades dancing on a whited canvass, and magnified into apparent life! – if thou art perfectly at leisure for such trivial amusement, walk in, and view the wonders of my Inchanted Garden.[15]

The two parts of *The Botanic Garden* are illustrated with numerous drawings of plants, but the most interesting illustrations are three engravings from designs by Henry Fuseli. At least one of the engravings was done by Blake, an illustration called the "Fertilization of Egypt"

---

[13] Hunt, p. 310.
[14] See Robert E. Schofield, *The Lunar Society of Birmingham* (Oxford: Oxford Univ. Press, 1963), pp. 422-23.
[15] Darwin, *The Botanic Garden*, part II, p. 9.

in the third canto of "The Economy of Vegetation." A recent article suggests that Blake designed part of the illustration as well, even though Fuseli's name is engraved on it, and in fact was impressed enough with Darwin's poem to remember it later when he was writing *Jerusalem*.[16] Blake did other engraving for Darwin's printer, J. Johnson, and probably other work on Darwin's books. Blake himself, of course, was a highly visual artist and he probably would have approved of Darwin's emphasis on the imaginative and artificial. But undoubtedly Blake also mocked Darwin's belief in a univocal world of matter, probably even in the old-man bearded figure of the "Fertilization of Egypt" illustration.[17] Blake was notorious for re-interpreting and mocking writers that he illustrated according to his own mystical system.

Henry Fuseli, however, who was Blake's friend was no mystic at all and much closer to Darwin in philosophic and aesthetic attitude.[18] In fact, the Fuseli illustrations are fine examples of visual, imaginative motion with no definite "meaning" at all. They fit well with Darwin's theory of the visual and grace his books effectively. (It is a shame that a modern edition of at least *The Botanic Garden* with the Fuseli illustrations has not yet been done.) Darwin appreciated Fuseli's power to stimulate imaginative motion, and writes associating him with Shakespeare, ". . . the daring pencil of Fuseli transports us beyond the boundaries of nature, and ravishes us with the charm of the most interesting novelty. And Shakespeare, who excels in all these together, so far captivates the spectator. . . ." [19] The frontispiece of *The Botanic Garden* is a Fuseli design entitled "Flora Attired by the Elements." It is an intricate, playful, almost surrealist design with little creatures part human part flower and large curving ladies of fashion. In its "busy-ness" it is very visual and reminds me of Fuseli's more famous *A Midsummer Night's Dream* painting.[20]

---

[16] Albert S. Roe, "The Thunder of Egypt – Blake and Erasmus Darwin," in Alvin H. Rosenfeld, ed., *William Blake Essays for S. Foster Damon* (Providence: Brown Univ. Press 1969), pp. 159-169.

[17] For further discussion of Blake's mockery of the univocal world view through his drawings and illustrations see W. J. T. Mitchell, "Poetic and Pictorial Imagination in Blake's *The Book of Urizen*," in *Eighteenth-Century Studies*, 3 (Fall, 1969), 83-107.

[18] Blake was an ardent defender of Fuseli, which may have made him sympathetic to Darwin since Darwin patronized Fuseli. In any case, Blake wrote, "the truth is, [Fuseli] is a hundred years beyond the present generation." To the Editor of the Monthly Magazine, 1806. In David V. Erdman, ed., *The Poetry and Prose of William Blake* (New York: Doubleday, 1965), p. 705. Could this apply to Darwin's impressionism as well?

[19] Darwin, *The Botanic Garden*, part II, p. 44.

[20] A modern art historian writes, "[Fuseli was] neither a mystic nor a man of religious ideas, but one in whom the Romantic passion for the strange, the violent,

Darwin's most famous patronage of Fuseli has to do with Fuseli's most well-known painting, "Nightmare," of 1782. Darwin refers to the painting in a typical passage of verse in "The Loves of the Plants," and most editions of the poem print a fine engraving of the work facing the passage. Darwin's verse is heavy with personification and visual reference intended to stimulate association and imaginative motion. It is significant that the subject is dreams which, as we have seen, are the prototype of involuntary motion and for Darwin an analogue to imaginative artistic experience. He makes the point in the passage that during dreams the "will" or voluntary motion is suspended (as Wordsworth wrote with much more spiritual "meaning," "Almost suspended, we are laid asleep / In body, and become a living soul").[21] Fuseli's painting shows a woman suffering from nightmare with a "Demon-ape" sitting on her heaving bosom and the horse, or nightmare, itself peering through the curtain. Darwin's verse describes her as well as the fantasies, or imaginative motions, going through her mind. It is all vivid and evocative of several senses in a primitive Keats-like manner. It "means" little, however, as both Fuseli and Darwin evoke fantasy demons that would not survive comparison. But there are the "looser analogies" of imagination, not the "stricter" ones of ratiocination, and it is a delightful description:

> So on his NIGHTMARE, through the evening fog,
> Flits the squab Fiend o'er fen, and lake, and bog;
> Seeks some love-wilder'd Maid with sleep oppress'd,
> Alights, and, grinning, sets upon her breast.
> – Such as of late, amid the murky sky,
> Was mark'd by FUSELI's poetic eye;
> Whose daring tints, with SHAKESPEARE's happiest grace,
> Gave to the airy phantom form and place. –
> Back o'er her pillow sinks her blushing head,
> Her snow-white limbs hang helpless from the bed;
> While with quick sighs, and suffocative breath,
> Her interrupted heart-pulse swims in death.
> – Then shrieks of captured towns, and widows' tears,
> Pale lovers stretch'd upon their blood-stain'd biers,
> The headlong precipice that thwarts her flight,

the dream-like, the scene of fantasy or horror. . . ." William Gaunt, *A Concise History of English Painting* (New York: Praeger, 1964), p. 144. See also Ian Jack, *Keats and the Mirror of Art* (Oxford: Oxford Univ. Press, 1967), p. 127. Jack links the interest in visual qualities in Keats and Fuseli.

[21] Wordsworth, "Tintern Abbey," ll. 45-46.

The trackless desert, the cold starless night,
And stern-eyed Murderer, with his knife behind,
In dread succession agonize her mind.
O'er her fair limbs convulsive tremors fleet,
Start in her hands, and struggle in her feet:
In vain to scream with quivering lips she tries,
And strains in palsied lids her tremulous eyes;
In vain she *wills* to run, fly, swim, walk, creep;
The WILL presides not in the bower of SLEEP.
– On her fair bosom sits the Demon-Ape
Erect, and balances his bloated shape;
Rolls in their marble orbs his Gorgon-eyes,
And drinks with leathern ears her tender cries.[22]

III

Dreams, such as the one above, are either boring in their predictable unpredictability or they are horrid to us because of their fickle randomness. In any case, dreams seem distinctly scary; and pure imaginative motion, the closest experience to dreams according to Darwin, similarly produces a desire for more abstract, "human" meaning. This is a familiar dilemma for Romantic poets out of which they made great literature: Wordsworth's tempered morality of the "Ode to Duty," Coleridge's several near-perfect poems about the curse of the imagination (the "flashing eyes and floating hair"), Keats' late aborted attempt to write philosophic poems, and Byron's comic, ironic switching back and forth from play to seriousness. Darwin, in my opinion, is closest to Byron because of the dominant characteristic of intricacy in tone. But Darwin, in fact, anticipates and plays out on a much lower level of literary excellence the whole Romantic dilemma of discovering and using the power of imagination while at the same time worrying over the need for "meaning." The Romantics found spiritual meaning paradoxically within the imagination itself. Darwin could not do that. But there were traditional "meanings."

For example, Darwin's visualism contains elements not only of the playful picturesque of the camera obscura and the expressive garden but also of the iconic, mythic and traditionally pictorial. Jean Hagstrum has shown exhaustively how prone 18th-century poetry was to the firmly

---

[22] Darwin, *The Botanic Garden*, part II, pp. 71-72. "The Loves of the Plants," canto III, 11 51-78.
[23] Jean H. Hagstrum, *The Sister Arts* (Chicago, Univ. of Chicago Press, 1958).

postured, wide-meaning, pictorial allegory; and Darwin points many fully draped figures of meaningful personifications in which the "meaning" seems to take precedence over the visual qualities.[23] Darwin also toys continually (toys indicates that finally I do not think he fully believes all this) with the meanings or myths and their pictorial expression. His poems contain many references to the mythographers: Jacob Bryant, *A New System; or, An Analysis of Antient Mythology* (1774-76) and William Warburton, *The Divine Legation of Moses* (1738-41), to Joseph Spence, *Polymetis: or, An Enquiry Concerning the Agreement Between the Works of the Roman Poets, and the Remains of the Antient Artists* (1747), and to Pierre Danet, *A Complete Dictionary of the Greek and Roman Antiquities* (1700). A typical example would be the following note about one of his pictorial descriptions suggested by an "ancient gem" and prints from it:

Fair Psyche. 1. 48. Described from an ancient gem, on a fine onyx, in possession of the Duke of Marlborough, of which there is a beautiful print in Bryant's Mythol. vol. ii. p. 392. And from another ancient gem of Cupid and Psyche embracing, of which there is a print in Spence's Polymetis, p. 82.[24]

The most extended example of Darwin's iconic pictorialism, his belief in traditional myths that have been passed on in pictures, is the structure of his last long poem, *The Temple of Nature* (1803). He says in the preface that the poem is a series of scenical representations of the mysteries of nature modeled on the ancient Greek Eleusinian Mysteries. The illustrations to the poem also are more iconic and traditionally meaningful than "Nightmare." One illustration in particular, the unveiling of the goddess Nature in the frontispiece by Fuseli, has a complex iconography derived from 18th century mythography that Irwin Primer recently traced in a convincing manner.[25] In fact, most recent scholarship on Darwin, little as it is, tends to "swallow" his stated belief in myth and the mystery religions. A very recent article (1971) concludes firmly that Darwin was positively influenced by Bishop Warburton and the other mythographer divines, that he believed in a kind of ancient, universal, human religion communicated through icons and pictures.[26] In fact, in my own earlier study of Darwin (my 1967 doctoral disser-

[24] Darwin, *The Botanic Garden*, part I, p. 103.
[25] Irwin Primer, "Erasmus Darwin's *Temple of Nature*: Progress, Evolution and the Eleusinian Mysteries," in *Journal of the History of Ideas*, 25 (January-March 1964), 58-76.
[26] Robert N. Ross, " 'To Charm Thy Curious Eye': Erasmus Darwin's poetry at the Vestibule of Knowledge," in *Journal of the History of Ideas*, 32 (July-Sept., 1971), 379-394.

tation) I followed suit and argued that he definitely believed in a few
mythic patterns communicated obliquely through images.[27]

There is no question that Darwin's poems are sprinkled with pictorial,
mythic references. But I would emphasize now their dynamic relationship with the other playful, speculative, and skeptical elements in his
writings. After reading Hume and noticing Darwin's many references
and similarities to him, it has become harder and harder for me to
believe that Darwin took Bishop Warburton completely seriously. And
yet there is also the continual "irritable reaching after fact and reason,"
as Keats said, because imaginative motion is chaos by itself. In short,
Darwin tempers his playfulness and skepticism with myth and iconic
images. They are part of the "amusing" play of mind, and should not
be excluded dogmatically – especially when they *may* lead toward firmer
analogies. Darwin knows that at present myths are loose analogies like
any other picturesque or amusing qualities, but for that reason they are
neither more nor less valuable. In my opinion, Darwin is less a believer
in myth than an "imaginative player" with belief. Thus his "Preface"
to *The Temple of Nature* does not read as seriously to me now as it once
did since I am much more sensitive now to Darwin's ironic retreats.
Darwin himself suggested that the language needed a new mark of
punctuation to indicate irony, and so I will quote his "Preface" with my
own italics to emphasize irony:

The Poem which is here offered to the Public, does not pretend to instruct by
deep researches reasoning; its aim is *simply to* amuse, by bringing distinctly to
the imagination the beautiful and sublime images of the operations of Nature, . . .

The Deities of Egypt, and afterwards of Greece and Rome, were derived from
men famous in those early times, as in the ages of hunting, pasturage, and agri-
culture. [the Euhemerist interpretation of myth which, of course, is the least
spiritual]. The histories of some of their actions recorded in Scripture, or celebrated in the heathen mythology, *are introduced, as the Author hopes, without
impropriety,* into his account of these remote periods of human society.

In the Eleusinian mysteries, the philosophy of the works of Nature, with the
origin and progress of society, *are believed to have been taught* by allegoric
scenery, explained by the Hierophant to the initiated, which gave rise to the
machinery of the following Poem.[28]

Earlier, in a long "Additional Note" to *The Botanic Garden*, he had
thoughtfully and scholarly (Darwin read extensively in many disciplines
from aesthetics to mineralogy) theorized about these same Eleusinian

---

[27] See my doctoral dissertation *The Poems of Erasmus Darwin*, Diss. Columbia
Univ. 1967.
[28] Erasmus Darwin, *The Temple of Nature* (New York: T. & J. Swords, 1804),
preface.

Mysteries. He got a good bit of his information from Warburton; but what, in fact, draws Darwin to this brand of "religious" discussion is that there is not much information and so a great deal of room for imaginative motion, for speculation and conjecture. The occasion for this discussion is Darwin's fascination with his friend Wedgwood's ceramic copies of the famous Barbarini, or Portland, Vase, a first century glass urn decorated with a carved glass frieze. Wedgwood had ingeniously invented a way to copy the vase in his ceramic Jasper Ware (another conjunction of technology and imaginative motion), and the art object which fascinated the 18th century "... is still an object in which unprejudiced eyes will find much beauty. Moreover, it is not beauty alone which has kept interest in it alive. The subject of its frieze is an enigma which has challenged and defied three centuries of classical scholarship. The virtuosity of its workmanship has inspired modern craftsmen, including the great Josiah Wedgwood, to imitation." [29] Darwin's long prose discussion of the vase is his most ambitious attempt to "believe" visual allegory. He begins:

Many opinions and conjectures have been published concerning the figures on this celebrated vase. Having carefully examined one of Mr. Wedgwood's beautiful copies of this wonderful production of art, I shall add one more conjecture to the number.... This subject appears to me to be well chosen, and the story to be finely told; and that it represents what in ancient times engaged the attention of philosophers, poets, and heroes; I mean a part of the Eleusinian mysteries.

These mysteries ... consisted of scenical exhibitions, representing and inculcating the expectation of a future life after death, and, on this account, were encouraged by the government....[30]

Seven pages later after he has assigned allegoric interpretations to each of the figures on the vase and cited many authorities on myth, there is still no certitude about the meaning of the little $9\frac{3}{4}$ inch art object except that it has generated a good deal of imaginative motion. Darwin prefers, I think, this kind of mysterious religion because it can leave him skeptical. One of the final sentences in his note on the vase seems to undercut with good-natured skepticism any certitude that his imaginative motion might have generated: "I beg leave to add, that it does not appear to have been uncommon amongst the ancients, to put alle-

[29] D. E. L. Haynes, *The Portland Vase* (London: The British Museum, 1964), p. 7. See also John Bedford, *Wedgwood Jasper Ware* (New York: Walker and Co., 1964). Bedford writes, "The subject seems to be as obscure as the origin of the vase itself; but the most commonly accepted interpretation of the two scenes shown is that they illustrate the courtship of Peleus, a King of Thessaly, and Thetis, one of the Nereids," p. 26.

[30] Darwin, *The Botanic Garden,* part I, pp. 197-98.

gorical figures on funeral vases." [31] The next "Additional Note" in his book is on coal. In other words, visual allegory is indeed one habit of thought that men have used, one pattern of animal motion that we might repeat.

IV

The habit of thought that Darwin preferred (although any habit of thought, of course, *can* be used by a skeptical mind) was voluntary "ratiocination" with strict analogies in order to triangulate as closely as possible the causes of things. He knew the power of imaginative motion, in fact, had helped to discover it; but he preferred voluntary motion. In terms of beauty and visual effects, Darwin followed closely the lead of earlier empirical aestheticians, such as Burke, who looked for purely objective explanations of the effects of visible objects on the mind. It is known that Burke influenced Fuseli, and we have seen how Darwin was fascinated by and tried to emulate in words Fuseli's "sublime terror." [32] But it was Burke's ideas on the sources of "the beautiful" in visible objects that led Darwin to one of his most convincing objectivist theories about the source of imaginative motion in our minds. Burke had argued that curving lines (and he is indebted partly to Hogarth for this idea) impress our minds as beautiful as well as anything we associate with self-propagation. Darwin combines and elaborates these two notions and derives a fairly plausible, if primitive, explanation of the continuing influence of childhood sexuality on our later tastes. The key passage in Burke stresses the importance for our sense of beauty of the shape of the female breast, but does not link it with childhood sexuality:

Observe that part of a beautiful woman where she is perhaps the most beautiful, about the neck and breasts; the smoothness; the softness; the easy and insensible swell; the variety of the surface, which is never for the smallest space the same; the deceitful maze, through which the unsteady eye slides giddily, without knowing where to fix, or whither it is carried. Is not this a demonstration of that change of surface continual and yet hardly perceptible at any point which forms one of the great constituents of beauty? (It gives me no small pleasure to find that I can strengthen my theory in this point, by the opinion of the very ingenious Mr. Hogarth; whose ideas of the line of beauty I take in general to be extremely just. . . .[33]

[31] *Ibid.,* p. 204.
[32] For Fuseli's interest in Burke's notion of the "sublime," see Burke, A *Philosophical Enquiry into the Origin of Our Ideas of the Sublime and Beautiful,* J. T. Boulton, eds. (Notre Dame: Univ. of Notre Dame Press, 1968), pp. cxiv-cxvi.
[33] *Ibid.,* p. 115. Part Three, section XV.

Darwin read both Hogarth's *Analysis of Beauty* (1753) and Burke although he gets a little confused and credits Hogarth with having emphasized the shape of the female breast whereas Hogarth had described only the serpentine line of beauty.[34] No matter, though, because Darwin went further than both men in speculating about a purely objective explanation of why we like particular artistic shapes – such as the curving shape of the Portland Vase even. His passage on the curving line of beauty and sex, as it appears in the section on "Instinct" in the *Zoonomia*, is well worth quoting entire. It reminds of the "first Affections" of Wordsworth's "Intimations Ode," and the two foreshadow Freud:

Our perception of beauty consists in our recognition, by the sense of vision, of those objects, first, which have before inspired our love by the pleasure which they have afforded to many of our senses; as to our sense of warmth, of touch, of smell, of taste, hunger and thirst; and, secondly, which bear any analogy of form to such objects.

When the babe, soon after it is born into this cold world, is applied to its mother's bosom, its sense of perceiving warmth is first agreeably affected; next its sense of smell is delighted with the odour of her milk; then its taste is gratified by the flavour of it; afterwards the appetites of hunger and of thirst afford pleasure by the possession of their objects, and by the subsequent digestion of the ailment; and lastly, the sense of touch is delighted by the softness and smoothness of the milky fountain, the source of such variety of happiness.

All these various kinds of pleasure at length become associated with the form of the mother's breast; which the infant embraces with its hands, presses with its lips, and watches with its eyes; and thus acquires more accurate ideas of the form of its mother's bosom, than of the odour and flavour, or warmth, which it perceives by its other senses. And hence, at our maturer years, when any object of vision is presented to us, which by its waving or spiral lines, bears any similitude to the form of the female bosom, whether it be found in a landscape with soft gradations of rising and descending surface, or in the forms of some antique vases, or in other works of the pencil or chisel, we feel a general glow of delight, which seems to influence all our senses; and, if the object be not too large, we experience an attraction to embrace it with our arms, and to salute it with our lips, as we did in our early infancy the bosom of our mother. And thus we find, according to the ingenious idea of Hogarth, that the waving lines of beauty were originally taken from the temple of Venus.

This animal attraction is love; which is a sensation, when the object is present; and a desire, when it is absent. Which constitutes the purest source of human felicity. The cordial drop in the otherwise vapid cup of life, and which overpays mankind for the care and labour, which are attached to the preeminence of his situation above other animals.[35]

[34] See James V. Logan, *The Poetry and Aesthetics of Erasmus Darwin* (Princeton, Princeton Univ. Press, 1936), p. 60.

[35] Erasmus Darwin, *Zoonomia; or The Laws of Organic Life,* First American edition (New York: T. & J. Swords, 1796), pp. 104-105. For a very recent discussion by a psychologist of the art of "beauty" as complexity (much animal motion)

Not only the curving line of beauty (whether it be seen in landscapes, vases, or women) but also sex itself derives much of its pleasure from its association with childhood sensation. In fact, as Darwin says at the end of the passage, life would be "vapid" if it were not for the animal motions of imagination and sex. Mythic meanings seem to be lost in this analysis. The breasts in the Fuseli frontispiece to *The Temple of Nature* are not so much mythic as they are just breasts; the Portland Vase is more curves than revelation. The several other Fuseli illustrations in Darwin's most mythic poem, allegedly modeled on the Eleusinian Mysteries, although they allegorize myths are most memorable for their depiction of voluptuous, shapely women. So it is not just childhood breast fixation that Darwin theorizes about, there is sex everywhere, of all varieties, throughout his poems in particular. In most cases, the tone is light and playful. Sex is fun and infinitely various. The structure of "The Loves of the Plants" is to tell one risqué story after another of the varied love life of plants personified. The theme spills over into the next poem, "The Economy of Vegetation," and the following note is a typical example of Darwin's playful tone:

Love out his hour. 1. 472. [Canto IV] The vegetable passion of love is agreeably seen in the flower of the parnassia, in which the males alternately approach and recede from the female; and in the flower of nigella, or devil in the bush, in which the tall females bend down to their dwarf husbands. But I was this morning surprised to observe, amongst Sir Brooke Boothby's valuable collection of plants at Ashbourn, the manifest adultery of several females of the plant Collinsonia, who had bent themselves into contact with the males of other flowers of the same plant in their vicinity, neglectful of their own.[36]

But sex is also a very serious and important matter to Darwin. He fathered fourteen children himself, and the subsequent Darwin lineage (blended with the Galtons) is an ideal example of the raw, yet subtle power of sexual genetics. Although he is certainly not writing about his own offspring – except insofar as we all write about our offspring when we write about the dynamics of life – Darwin came close to uncovering and celebrating the real role of sexual reproduction in the improvement of species. He argued that sexual reproduction (uniting two individuals) was the most highly developed kind of reproduction because it allowed for the blending of characteristics. The second canto of *The Temple of Nature* is a long celebration of this supreme accomplishment of nature

that mentions Hogarth's line of beauty see Rudolf Arnheim, *Entropy and Art* (Berkeley, Univ. of Calif. Press, 1971), p. 51. For a Renaissance influence on the line of beauty, see Hagstrum, *The Sister Arts,* pp. 169-170.

[36] Darwin, *The Botanic Garden,* part I, p. 121.

(which he also describes in the *Zoonomia*) and, although he never elaborates the details of evolution and genetics, he is close to the theory. The following lines of verse describe first reproduction without sex (where also, incidentally, there are no breasts, "Beauty's orbs") and then nature's development of sex in order to give pleasure and improvement:

> III. "In these lone births no tender mothers blend
> Their genial powers to nourish or defend;
> No nutrient streams from Beauty's orbs improve
> These orphan babes of solitary love;
> Birth after birth the line unchanging runs,
> And fathers live transmitted in their sons;
> Each passing year beholds the unvarying kinds,
> The same their manners, and the same their minds.
> Till, as ere long successive buds decay,
> And insect-shoals successive pass away,
> Increasing wants the pregnant parents vex
> With the fond wish to form a softer sex;
> Whose milky rills with pure ambrosial food
> Might charm and cherish their expected brood.
> The potent wish, in the productive hour,
> Calls to its aid Imagination's power,
> O'er embryon throngs with mystic charm presides,
> And sex from sex the nascent world divides,
> With soft affections warms the callow trains,
> And gives to laughing Love his nymphs and swains;
> Whose mingling virtues interweave at length
> The mother's beauty with the father's strength.[37]

One of the footnotes to these lines deals with an eccentric theory of Darwin's, which later science has not borne out, about male dominance in reproduction through the imagination. Apparently, this was a fairly common notion in the 18th century. Tristram Shandy's father held it as did Linnaeus. But Darwin seems to stretch the notion as far as it will go, and his theorizing about the power of imagination in sex seems to me to be a strong indication of his univocal, materialist philosophy and aesthetic. Even though the idea has proved wrong, it is a good sign of the way Darwin saw the world – of a piece. Often wrong theories tell us more about an individual's philosophic position than right ones – theories such as Newton's theory of the aether. In any case, for Darwin imagi-

---

[37] Darwin, *The Temple of Nature*, pp. 45-46.

native motion operates both in the sphere of dreams and art, and in the sphere of sexual reproduction. The note reads:

Imagination's power, 1. 118. The manner in which the similarity of the progeny to the parent, and the sex of it, are produced by the power of imagination, is treated of in *Zoonomia,* Sect. XXXIX. 6. 3. It is not to be understood, that the first living fibres which are to form an animal, are produced by imagination, with any similarity of form to the future animal; but with appetencies or propensities, which shall produce by accretion of parts the similarity of form and feature, or of sex, corresponding with the imagination of the father.[38]

The reference to the *Zoonomia* is to the section on "Generation" in which most of Darwin's early theory of biological evolution appears. What is important for our consideration is the role that "imagination" plays in this obviously physical process of generation. And since it plays such a major role, we can be certain that Darwin considers it a physical force. One attribute of a physical force is that it can be managed, controlled, in fact, trained; and Darwin wrote daringly about training the imagination to produce certain effects in sexual reproduction just as earlier he had written confidently about achieving certain visual and synesthetic imaginative motions with machines. In general, the joyous use of the body-mind machine for its own sake seems to be a key characteristic of the literature of sensibility, of valueless motion. A provocative recent article in a collection on sensibility discusses the sexuality of *Fanny Hill* in a very serious, yet playful way, associating it with the materialism of La Mettrie whose dominant metaphor, the article notes, for the operation of the mind is the sexual metaphor.[39] Similarly, Darwin relates sex and mind in a reciprocal relationship that makes sex imaginative at the same time that mind becomes clearly physical. The non-traditional implications of this probably account for the continual ironic tone. The following two paragraphs from the *Zoonomia* are not as playfully ironic as is usual in Darwin, even in this scientific treatise (recall his discussion of breasts above), but they are daringly "hushed" and slightly secretive because the information they convey is so non-traditional:

   3. I conclude, that the imagination of the male, at the time of copulation, or at the time of the secretion of the semen, may so affect this secretion by irritative or sensitive association ... as to cause the production of similarity of form and of features, with the distinction of sex; as the motions of the chissel of the turner imitate or correspond with those of the ideas of the artist. . . .

   [38] Darwin, p. 46n.
   [39] Leo Braudy, "Fanny Hill and Materialism," in *Eighteenth-Century Studies,* 4 (Fall, 1970), 21-40.

7. Hence I conclude, that the act of generation cannot exist without being accompanied with ideas, and that a man must have at that time either a general idea of his own male form, or of the form of his male organs; or an idea of the female form, or of her organs; and that this marks the sex, and the peculiar resemblances of the child to either parent. From whence it would appear, that the phalli, which were hung round the necks of the Roman ladies, or worn in their hair, might have effect in producing a greater proportion of male children; and that the calipaedia, or art of begetting beautiful children, and of procreating either males or females, may be taught by affecting the imagination of the male-parent; that is, by the fine extremities of the seminal glands imitating the actions of the organs of sense, either of sight or touch. But the manner of accomplishing this cannot be unfolded with sufficient delicacy for the public eye, but may be worth the attention of those who are seriously interested in the procreation of a male or female child.[40]

These mysteries of controlling animal motion are the only mysteries that Darwin really believes in.

But for Darwin sex works not only on the small level of animal repro-duction, but also on the cosmic level of creation – at least metaphorically. One of his most admired paragraphs of verse combines images of curving female bosoms, bursting eggs, and interstellar creation. These are the loose analogies of the imagination, of course, but since the imagination has a viable physical base the images at least tell us about motion. The passage is from early in the first canto of "The Economy of Vegetation":

When LOVE DIVINE, with brooding wings unfurl'd,
Call'd from the rude abyss the living world
" – LET THFRE BE LIGHT!" proclaim'd the ALMIGHTY LORD,
Astonish'd Chaos heard the potent word; –
Through all his realms the kindling Ether runs,
And the mass starts into a million suns;
Earths round each sun with quick explosions burst,
And second planets issue from the first;
Bend, as they journey with projectile force,
In bright ellipses their reluctant course;
Orbs wheel in orbs, round centres centres roll,
And form, self-balanced, one revolving whole.
– Onward they move amid their bright abode,
Space without bound, THE BOSOM OF THEIR GOD! [41]

Shortly after the poem was published Horace Walpole wrote to a friend, ". . . the twelve verses that by miracle describe and comprehend the creation of the universe out of chaos, are in my opinion the most sublime

---

[40] Darwin, *Zoonomia*, pp. 383. 378.
[41] Darwin, *The Botanic Garden*, part I, pp. 9-10.

passage in any author." [42] Darwin had pleased a dilettante of the picturesque with bursting curves, cosmic sexuality, and terrifying sublimity all
lumped together in a glittering passage about motion.

V

If the taste of the late 18th century confused and overlapped Burke's
careful categories of the sublime and the beautiful, Darwin certainly was
no exception because his ideas on visualism and mental activity in
general led toward the conclusion, as we have seen, that matter in motion
was responsible for all effects. Animal motion, it is true, was of different
kinds. But powerful, continuous animal motion, which is the involuntary
kind since we know that reason is sporadic, is all that is necessary to
produce any of the imaginative categories that aestheticians might distinguish as sublime or beautiful or picturesque. Darwin is finally such a
complete materialist that he is skeptical of the aesthetic categories, and
opts simply for monistic motion. Here is what he says on the categories:

Objects of taste have been generally divided into the beautiful, the sublime, and
the new; and lately to these have been added the picturesque. The beautiful, so
well explained in Hogarth's analysis of beauty, consists of curved lines and smooth
surfaces, ... any object larger than usual, as a very large temple or a very large
mountain, gives us the idea of sublimity; with which is often confounded the
terrific and the melancholic: what is now termed picturesque, includes objects
which are principally neither sublime nor beautiful, but which, by their variety
and intricacy, joined with a due degree of regularity or uniformity, convey to the
mind an agreeable sentiment of novelty. Many other agreeable sentiments may
be excited by visible objects; thus to the sublime and beautiful may be added the
terrific, tragic, melancholic, artless, etc. while novelty superinduces a charm upon
them all.[43]

When the categories proliferate as they do at the end of the above, then
none of them become meaningful and all that is left is the excited animal
motion from visible objects.

But for the "Picturesque Moment," as Martin Price calls it, motion
for its own sake is sufficient. It can be lively and spiraling. It can be
sexually playful, and most of all it can be continually growing. One of
the genuinely appealing characteristics of Darwin's position is its vitality.
Motion, curving movement, subsumes everything. And until one begins
to think about it, quantity becomes sufficient for happiness. Tension in
Darwin comes, of course, when he does think about "value," but the

---

[42] To Thomas Barrett, May 14, 1792. In Horace Walpole, *The Letters of* . . . ,
Mrs. Paget Toynbee, ed. (Oxford, Oxford Univ. Press, 1905), XV, 110.
[43] Darwin, *The Temple of Nature*, pp. 84n-85n.

drift of all his ideas is toward the power of continual motion – quantified happiness. Toward the end of *The Temple of Nature,* he considers the role of death in the scheme of things, and describes it as just an addition to continuing motion. A note reads:

The sum total of the happiness or organized nature is probably increased rather than diminished, when one large old animal dies and is converted into many thousand young ones; which are produced or supported, with their numerous progeny, by the same organic matter. Linnaeus asserts, that three of the flies called musca vomitoria, will consume the body of a dead horse as soon as a lion can.[44]

Another note a little later in *The Temple of Nature* on "happiness" conveys beautifully Darwin's vitality and what is almost finally a belief in motion for its own sake:

... hence the quantity or number of organized bodies, and their improvement in size, as well as their happiness, has been continually increasing, along with the solid parts of the globe; and will probably continue to increase till the whole terraqueous sphere, and all that inhabit it, shall dissolve by a general conflagration, and be again reduced to their elements.

Thus all the suns, and the planets which circle round them, may again sink into one central chaos; and may again, by explosions, produce a new world; which, in process of time, may resemble the present one, and at length again undergo the same catastrophe! These great events may be the result of the immutable laws impressed on matter by the Great Cause of Causes, Parent of Parents, Ens Entium! [45]

Darwin's picturesque visualism is a continual voyaging in an age of voyages, a preparation perhaps in imaginative animal motion for the voyages of his more famous grandson.[46] There is another note in *The Botanic Garden* describing a walking trip up a hill outside Lichfield to observe the moon and the mist. It reminds me of Wordsworth's description near the end of *The Prelude* of his climb up Mt. Snowdon. But Darwin's hike trails off into other references and other observations. It is too peripheral, too circling and has no center. Darwin's is a voyage for its own sake, and, unlike Wordsworth, he never breaks through, or even seems to want to break through, to a spot of time:

[44] *Ibid.,* p. 127n.
[45] *Ibid.,* p. 130n.
[46] In the special issue on "Sensibility" of *Eighteenth-Century Studies* there is a very definite connection made between sea exploration of the time and the mental voyaging of sensibility. See Donald Davie, "John Ledyard: The American Traveler and his Sentimental Journeys," in *ECS,* 4 (Fall, 1970), 57-70. Also, Darwin himself apparently wrote much of Anna Seward's *Elegy on Captain Cook.* See Margaret Ashmun, *The Singing Swan* (1931; rpt. New York: Greenwood, 1968), p. 76.

On ascending up the side of a hill from a misty valley, I have observed a beautiful coloured halo round the moon, when a certain thickness of mist was over me,
which ceased to be visible as soon as I emerged out of it; and well remember
admiring, with other spectators, the shadow of the three spires of the cathedral
church at Lichfield, the moon rising behind it, apparently broken off, and lying
distinctly over our heads, as if horizontally on the surface of the mist, which
arose about as high as the roof of the church. There are some curious remarks
on shadows, or reflections seen on the surface of mists from high mountains, in
Ulloa's Voyages. The dry mist of summer 1783, was probably occasioned by
volcanic eruption, as mentioned in note on Chunda, vol. ii ["The Loves of the
Plants"] and, therefore, more like the atmosphere of smoke, which hangs, on
still days, over great cities.[47]

[47] Darwin, *The Botanic Garden,* part I, p. 46n.

CHAPTER FOUR

MAKING IT STRANGE TECHNICALLY

[he] wrote his couplet yearly to the spring,
As dissertation of profound delight . . .
Sonorous nutshells rattling inwardly.

Wallace Stevens,
"The Comedian as the Letter C"

I

As one would expect from Darwin after knowing his physiological and univocal theories, the couplet art that he practiced was blatant aestheticism – artificial, technically intricate, and very much removed from everyday life. Like modern Formalists, Darwin is continually conscious of what is "literary" about literature, and takes great pains to thicken the language of his couplets. Ironically, the weakest thing in much of his couplet art is that he chooses word patterns and "devices" that are not artificial enough in the sense that by the time he uses them they are too familiar as thickening devices for poetic language. Again, what is most interesting, though, is his theory and the problems it created for his art because his problems are still to a great extent our problems. The Russian Formalist and American New Criticism movements have produced a theory of literature based on the "scientific" study of taste and imaginative motion much more sophisticated and various than Darwin's, but with some of the same problems. This makes his early ratiocinations all the more important for study.

Perhaps literature needs spiritual illusions, large anthropocentric humanness, in order to avoid the self-fulfilling prophecy of meaninglessness and despair associated with rigorous analysis. Aesthetic engineering and technical virtuosity, even at its best, is still valueless – except in some paradoxical, Humean way that says we can trust nature to provide all the mental apparatus we need as a species. In fact, the major assumption behind 20th-century Formalism and New Criticism is that what our species needs and responds to in art is "strangeness." [1] This emphasis

---

[1] See Lee T. Lemon and Marion J. Reis, eds., *Russian Formalist Criticism, Four Essays* (Lincoln: University of Nebraska Press, 1965), and Rene Wellek and Austin Warren, *Theory of Literature* (New York: Harcourt, Brace, 1956).

on "making it strange" recalls Darwin's conclusions about novelty as the prime stimulus for involuntary imaginative motion. In any case, Darwin and our recent theorists are in agreement that the language of poetry is different from everyday language. W. K. Wimsatt, who carries on the tradition of technical analysis from earlier in the century if not its "scientific" disregard for meaning, sounds much like Darwin writing in the "Interludes" to "The Loves of the Plants":

There is a one-way transparent intellectual reference [in prose, strict analogy]. But poetry by thickening the medium increases the disparity between itself and its referents.[2]

The term "Formalist" interestingly enough applies also to those thinkers in physics and mathematics who subscribe to a theory of indeterminacy:

The Formalist believes that mathematics is pure form. . . . For a Formalist the question of whether . . . is as meaningless as is, for a physicist such as Bohr, the question of whether or not an electron "really" has an exact simultaneous position and velocity.[3]

One follower of Russian literary Formalism explains so explicitly that taste is relative and changing as a result of either its strangeness or familiarity that we sense a hint that even Darwin's "bad poems" may undergo a revival when their particular kind of "badness" becomes less familiar. In fact, one of the very things that was too familiar about Darwin's poems for Wordsworth, their use of the heroic couplet, may seem strange enough now to be of interest. In any case, a strict Formalist would not rule out any possibility for shifting values in art:

How far can this criterion carry us? As applied by the Russians, it is admittedly relativist. There is no aesthetic norm, says Mukarovsky, for it is the essence of the aesthetic norm to be broken. No poetic style stays strange. Hence, Mukarovsky argues, works can lose their aesthetic function and then later, perhaps, regain it – after the too familiar becomes again unfamiliar. In the case of specific poems, we all know what it is to "use them up," temporarily. Sometimes we later come back to them, again and again; sometimes we appear to have exhausted them. So, as literary history moves on, some poets grow strange again, others remain "familiar." [4]

It is a waste of time to try to decide whether it is valuable to have value judgments. Locke's method, Darwin's method, and the method of

---

[2] W. K. Wimsatt, Jr., *The Verbal Icon, Studies in the Meaning of Poetry* (New York: Anchor, 1965), p. 217.
[3] Lynn Arthur Steen, "New Models of the Real-Number Line," in *Scientific American*, 225 (August, 1971), 99.
[4] Wellek and Warren, p. 242.

Formalism are all intended as ways to make "modest" discoveries and theoretical suggestions of how things work under the assumption that we must know how things work in detail before we can know how they work *in toto*. The sophistry, of course, is that in order to sort out details theories are needed; and the best theories work comprehensively. But nevertheless, the test of theory is in detail.

The work of the Formalists on the details of meter in poetry (something that is distinctly a poetic detail as even Wordsworth concludes) led in two directions. On one hand, the linguists have attempted to discover a "natural" meter is poetic language while, on the other hand, the New Critics are interested in the purely literary complexity of literary language – what can be artificially made strange. Darwin, like many of the Romantics, anticipated both aspects of this detailed interest in prosody.

II

Wimsatt and Monroe Beardsley have recently made a valuable definition of the two basic kinds of metrical pattern in English. They distinguish between what they call "strong-stress" meter, in which the metrical pattern is determined solely by the pattern of stresses, or heavily accented syllables, and "syllable-stress" meter, in which all of the syllables, unstressed as well as stressed, are taken into account when determining the metrical pattern. The latter is more artificial and less attuned to speech rhythms. For this reason Wimsatt and Beardsley prefer it over the "strong-stress" meter as a poetic form. It is closer to the Formalists' theory of making language "strange" in order to stimulate, in Darwin's term, "imaginative motion." They conclude:

where syllable-stress meters lose in freedom and naturalness of speech feeling, they gain in the possibility of precise interplay. Perhaps this suggests a reason why the greatest English poetry (Chaucer, Shakespeare, Milton, Pope, Wordsworth) has after all been written in the more artful syllable-stress meter – not in the older, simpler, more directly natural strong-stress meter.[5]

Since the greatest artificiality in a syllable-stress meter derives from the mere counting, or numbering, of the syllables, this practice of counting is apt to become the major criterion for verse among writers who want regular formal patterns, who are interested in the word as "word." Such

---

[5] W. K. Wimsatt, Jr. and Monroe C. Beardsley, "The Concept of Meter: An Exercise in Abstraction," in *PMLA*, 74 (1959), 597. This essay has been reprinted by Wimsatt in his book *Hateful Contraries* (Lexington: University of Kentucky Press, 1965), pp. 108-145.

an extreme devotion to the artificial pattern occurred in English literature during the Augustan Age, when some metrists preferred to call the iambic pentameter line a decasyllabic line, thus paying more attention to the number of syllables than to the stresses on the syllables when they are pronounced. A symptom of this preference is the name for meter that was common at the time, "numbers." In Paul Fussell's valuable description of this theory of meter and of the changes that it went through in the 18th century, he says that the Augustan metrists, in addition to subscribing to a highly artificial description of meter, also felt that a poet should work in only one meter.[6]

Erasmus Darwin agreed with the Augustans on the latter point, and he worked in only one meter, the heroic couplet. But he differed from them in his description of meter. The change in metrical principles during the 18th century, as Fussell describes it, was toward less artificiality. The end product of this change was the strong-stress meter of Coleridge's *Christabel,* in which the number of syllables in a line is unimportant, and the meter is an attempt to suggest speech rhythms. For the study of Darwin, however, it is necessary to consider a metrical pattern midway between the syllable counting of the early Augustans and the near speech rhythms of Coleridge. In describing such a pattern, it is impossible to avoid some mention of that bug-bear of English prosody: the metrical foot.[7] Fussell says that a strict syllable-counter in the 18th century, such as Samuel Johnson, only allowed two metrical feet in English verse, the iamb and the trochee.[8] The tri-syllabic feet, the anapest and the dactyl, were anathema to syllable counters because such feet tend to weaken the regular alternation of stresses that both Pope and Johnson knew as "harmony." [9] This was not a simple attitude toward meter, because it did allow, indeed require, variation, and the fact that any variation had to take place within the strict confines of a highly arbitrary pattern was actually an assertion of great complexity, of what Wimsatt and Beardsley call "interplay." Fussell interprets the metrical theories of these syllabists as an attempt to assert the difference between verse and ordinary linguistic phenomena, and thus more fully to control language. He writes:

[6] Paul Fussell, Jr., *Theory of Prosody in Eighteenth-Century England* (New London: Connecticut College, 1954), p. 43.

[7] In a more general account of meter, Fussell writes: Because the idea of the foot has been imported into modern accentual-syllabic scansion from classical quantitative practice, quarrels about its nature and even its existence have been loud and long since the Renaissance. Paul Fussell, Jr., *Poetic Meter and Poetic Form* (New York: Random House, 1965), p. 23.

[8] Fussell, *Theory of Prosody . . .* , p. 25.

[9] *Ibid.,* p. 8.

Perhaps [syllabist] prosody may some day gain our respect for its uncompromising assertion of the power of the mind to control experience, and for its human conviction of the dignity of that power.[10]

Darwin inherited many of the assumptions underlying metrical artificiality from the Augustans, but he also inherited the theory and practice of tri-syllabic substitution, that is, the use of an anapest or dactyl in the place of an iamb or trochee. Fussell argues that these substitutions became acceptable primarily through the development of the analogies between poetry and music that fascinated 18th-century writers. By the end of the century, it was a commonplace among metrists that:

... since a musical bar may contain an infinite *number* of notes as long as its *time* is equal to that of the other bars in the same sequence, a foot modelled on its musical analogus may also contain a varied *number* of syllables as long as its *time* is equal to that of each surrounding foot. [italics his] [11]

Darwin's theory on meter is relevant here because he tried to support the poetry and music analogy, and this attempt provided him with the necessary assumptions to allow free tri-syllabic substitution in his verse. On the other hand, Darwin never goes so far as to consider meter other than artificial pattern. In the first interlude of "The Loves of the Plants," he suggests that the oral presentation of poetry, that is the physical language experience, can help little in comprehending the meter:

... some prose has its melody; and even measure. And good verses, well spoken in a language unknown to the hearer, are not easily to be distinguished from good prose.[12]

Then in the third interlude, he tries his hand at inventing a new method of scansion. The result is a consistent, yet dismaying, example of abstracting a pattern from the words. Just as the scansion of the modern linguists is impractical because it notices too many variations in the physical reality of sound, so Darwin's scansion is impractical because it abstracts too complex a system.

He proposes the entire couplet as the basic unit in scansion, and says that the iambic couplet should be divided into five bars containing three equal time units apiece, each unit analogous to a "crotchet," or quarter note, in music. Thus a couplet of twenty syllables would contain the equivalent of fifteen quarter notes. When Darwin explains that a weak

---

[10] *Ibid.,* p. 67.
[11] *Ibid.,* p. 109. Fussell calls the theorists who held this theory "bar-foot analogists." The most important of these were Charles Gildon, Samuel Say, John Mason, Joshua Steele, and William Mitford.
[12] Erasmus Darwin, *The Botanic Garden, Part II,* fifth edition (London: J. Johnson, 1799), pp. 61-62.

stress is equal in time to one half a strong stress, his counting becomes clear. Over two lines, his scheme always gives him the equivalent of ten stressed and ten unstressed syllables (or fifteen quarter notes); but the stresses do not have to come alternately; nor do there even have to be ten strong stresses in each unit since he counts "rests." Thus his scheme allows him to include more tri-syllabic substitution while still maintaining that he follows an artificial symmetry.

In addition to equating iambic couplets with triple time in music, Darwin equates dactylic or anapestic meters with duple time. It would seem to be just the other way around, but in both cases the abstract scheme "counts out" as Darwin explains it. I will not go further with his explanation of duple time since it does not apply to his own practice in verse, but the following passage will illustrate his bizarre scansion of an iambic couplet. The couplet is his own, and he later uses it near the end of "The Economy of Vegetation." He also uses it again with slight variation near the end of The Temple of Nature:

> 3 Life buds or breathes / from Indus to / the poles,
> 4 And the / vast surface kind / les, as it rolls. /

In these lines there is a quaver [eighth note] and a crotchet alternately in the first bar; a quaver, two crotchets, and a quaver, make the second bar. In the third bar there is a quaver, a crotchet, and a rest after the crotchet, that is after the word *poles,* and two quavers begin the next line. The fourth bar consists of quavers and crotchets alternately. In the last bar there is a quaver, and a rest after it, viz. after the word *kindles*; and then two quavers and a crotchet. You will clearly perceive the truth of this, if you prick the musical characters above mentioned under the verses.[13]

Because Darwin tries to justify what is nearly a strong-stress meter by an appeal to an artificial pattern, I conclude that in theory he is midway between the extreme artificiality of the syllable-counters (who were syllable-stress metrists with very little stress on stress) and the preference for "naturalness" of the Romantic strong-stress metrists, principally Coleridge. His verse can be scanned, therefore, in an accordingly halfway manner. The long passages that are scanned first are scanned simply for the strong stresses; but it is also possible to document, as I do later, Darwin's more conservative syllable-stress foot substitution. Although he had a divided mind on theories of meter, some of Darwin's metrical practice seems fairly successful.

In the following passage, for example, if we scan simply for strong stresses, we find variation in the number of them per line:

13 *Ibid.,* p. 175.

Rocks rear'd on rocks in huge disjointed piles
Form the tall turrets, and the lengthen'd ailes:
Broad ponderous piers sustain the roof, and wide
Branch the vast rain-bow ribs from side to side.
While from above descends in milky streams
One scanty pencil of illusive beams,
Suspended crags and gaping gulfs illumes,
And gilds the horrors of the deepen'd glooms.[14]

Only two of the eight lines have the traditional five stresses, while each line but one contains ten syllables. The word "ponderous" is tri-syllabic because Darwin would probably not have felt the need for elision, as I explain in a moment. In this passage, the stress variations help the image of the cave: the six-stress lines describing the wide roof of the cave are opposed to the four-stress lines that describe the thin beam of light.

In the use of metrical variation, Darwin is a skillful imitator of Pope with one additional characteristic. Since he had no theoretical reason to avoid either hiatus or tri-syllabic feet as Pope did, there were more possibilities for variation open to him.[15] Anna Seward noticed the most common type of metrical variation, the substitution of a trochee for an iamb in the first foot. She writes:

The Darwinian peculiarity is in part formed by the very frequent use of the imperative mood, generally beginning the couplet either with that, or with the verb active, or the noun personal. Hence, the accent lies oftener on the first syllable of each couplet in his verse than in that of any other rhymist; . . .[16]

The initial trochee is probably the most common variation among all 18th century couplet writers, and it would be fruitless to try to prove or disprove Miss Seward's quantitative conclusion. It is more relevant, I

[14] *Ibid.*, Canto III, 11. 93-100. I realize, of course, that the linguists distinguish four degrees of stress, but rather agree with John Crowe Ransom that the linguistic approach by implication posits even more degrees of stress in any given reading while the abstract pattern requires the simpler distinction between stress and lack of stress. See Ransom, "The Strange Music of English Verse," in *Kenyon Review*, 18 (Summer, 1956), 460-477.

[15] The elisions which Pope used to avoid hiatus, or vowel gaping, would necessarily reduce the number of tri-syllabic feet for their own sake. See discussion of syllabists earlier.

[16] Anna Seward, *Memoirs of the Life of Dr. Darwin* (London: J. Johnson, 1804), pp. 180-181.

think, to illustrate particular variations in order to show that Darwin's verse can be scanned for foot substitution as well as simply for the strong stresses.

In the following description of *Amaryllis formosissima,* a plant related to the lilies, three of the five lines begin with trochees, two of which are a result of beginning the line with an active verb; the other trochee is created by the use of an expression similar to a personal noun, "*six* rival youths," in which the number is italicized since it is important to the Linnean categories. The plant has a bell-shaped flower to protect its sexual parts: six stamens and one pistil. Darwin personifies this fact into one of the many "touching" little scenes that make his poems so artificial and comic. The lines are a good example of the frequent use of the initial trochee:

> $\quad\quad\quad\quad\overset{\circ\quad\circ\quad/}{}$
> Fair Amaryllis flies the incumbent storm,
> $\overset{/}{}$
> Seeks with unsteady step the shelter'd vale,
> And turns her blushing beauties from the gale. –
> $\overset{/}{}$
> *Six* rival youths, with soft concern impress'd,
> $\overset{/}{}$
> Calm all her fears, and charm her cares to rest. –[17]

The first line of the above quotation contains a tri-syllabic foot (which I have indicated with scansion marks). The frequency of tri-syllabic substitution in Darwin's couplets is the major metrical factor distinguishing them from Pope's couplets. There are three ways that tri-syllabic feet, which were forbidden by critical theory to the earlier writers of the heroic couplet, enter Darwin's verse. The first of these is represented above, where the phrase "the incumbent" includes a juxtaposition of vowels, or hiatus, which Pope would have probably eliminated by eliding the first two syllables, "th'incumbent." This would also eliminate, of course, the tri-syllabic foot. In addition to reducing the number of tri-syllabic feet by avoiding hiatus, the earlier couplet writers avoided tri-syllabic feet in general by means of two other kinds of elision that Darwin did not use. The first of these is the omission of vowels within words to reduce tri-syllables to di-syllables, such as the reduction of "wandering" to "wand'ring." The other is the elision of adjoining vowels within words, again to reduce tri-syllables to di-syllables, such as the

---

[17] Darwin, "The Loves of the Plants," canto I, 11. 152-156. Whenever I find it necessary to scan a line (if it is obviously iambic, I do not scan), I will use traditional scansion primarily because it works so well with Darwin's verse.

elision of the last two vowels in "indian." [18] Since Darwin held no objection to tri-syllabic feet, he did not practice any of these forms of
elision. His avoidance of the third form of elision, synaeresis, cannot be
known definitely since it is a matter of pronunciation and is never indicated on the page; but I suggest that his marked fondness for tri-syllabic
feet would have induced him to pronounce all of the syllables in a word
such as "indian,' or at least to tend toward a tri-syllabic pronunciation.

The following two couplete illustrate this fondness for tri-syllabic feet
and also show how they can be used by Darwin for expressive purposes.

> Your lucid banks condense with fingers chill
> ○   /   ○   / ○○   ○   ○ / ○   /
> The blue mist hovering round the gelid hill.[19]
> Round his large limbs were wound a thousand strings,
> ○ ○   ○   ○ /   ○ ○ / ○   ○   /
> By the weak hands of Confessors and Kings;[20]

In the first example, the Botanic Goddess is speaking to the "element"
of water and describing hovering mist on a cold day. Although there is
a light or "metrical" stress on the word "round," the impression of the
second line is that of two tri-syllabic feet back to back in the middle of
the line. Technically, I would call the first foot of the second line an
amphibrach with heaviest stress on the color image; then a dactyl, then
an anapest, and finally an iamb make up the rest of the line. The overall
impression of the line, however, is that of tri-syllabic substitution expressive of the image of the mist. The second line of the second couplet
becomes so involved with substitution for expressive purposes that there
is no iambic foot in the line at all. The first line is also an example of
initial trochaic substitution. The Botanic Goddess is describing the
Gulliver-like binding of the Giant, France, and in the second line, the
firm iambic pattern breaks down so that it scans as a pyrrhic foot followed by a spondee then two anapests. This seems expressive of the general
weakness of the French government, according to Darwin, just before
the Revolution.

Finally, I will quote a passage that uses tri-syllabic substitution to

---

[18] In other words, Darwin's tri-syllabic substitutions are sometimes merely a
matter of spelling. But spelling does often indicate pronunciation. Other tri-
syllabic substitutions are decidedly not merely the spelling out of previous dropped
syllables. See examples in the text. The elision of vowels between two words is
called "apocope." The omission of a vowel within a word is called "syncope."
And the elision of adjoining vowels within words is called "synaeresis." For the
classification of these figures in Renaissance rhetoric, see Sister Miriam Joseph,
Rhetoric in Shakespeare's Time (New York: Harcourt, Brace, 1962).

[19] Darwin, "The Economy of Vegetation," canto III, 11. 19-20.

[20] *Ibid.*, canto II, 11. 379-80.

suggest how sympathetic Darwin was with the metrical innovations that were leading to the breakup of the strict-syllabic regularity of the Augustans. According to the most strict syllabic-counters, the line of the heroic couplet could have no more than ten syllables and could have no tri-syllabic feet. Samuel Say, one of the metrists who contributed to the refutation of this theory, manufactured a couplet that became famous, according to Paul Fussell, among the advocates of tri-syllabic substitution. Fussell quotes the couplet in his history of this metrical change:

> O   / O O/ O   O   / O O /   O O /
> And many an amorous, many a humorous Lay,
> O   /   O O /   O   /   O / O O /
> Which many a Bard had chanted many a Day.[21]

Although both lines have only five stresses, the first line has fourteen syllables and the second twelve. In telling the story of a young couple whose house burns down with them in it on their wedding night, Darwin writes a line that may be indebted to Say's lone couplet. Darwin wants his readers to have a good leisurely cry, and the long line of tri-syllabic substitution is expressive here of languorous emotion. I quote four lines from the passage. The first three are regular (with two initial trochees), but the last line includes three anapests and thirteen syllables:

> The blushing Bride with wild disorder'd charms
> /
> Round her fond lover winds her ivory arms;
> /
> Beat as they clasp, their throbbing hearts with fear,
> O   / O O / O   / O O   / O O /
> And many a kiss is mixed with many a tear.[22]

After all these illustrations of Darwin's use of the late 18th-century Popean couplet have been noted, however, his most successful passages metrically are best scanned simply by marking the strong stresses. When this is done, we find that he does often begin with the "trochaic" strong stress; but more significantly many of his lines contain only four strong stresses. This characteristic, combined with medial caesura, creates the effect of balance or circularity. In the following passage of eighteen lines, I scan nine lines as containing only four strong stresses. There are eight lines with an initial strong stress:

> /   /   /   /
> Nurs'd by warm sun-beams in primeval caves
> /   /   /   /   /
> Organic Life began beneath the waves.

21 Fussell, *Theory of Prosody* ..., p. 116.
22 Darwin, "The Economy of Vegetation," canto III, 11. 437-440.

First Heat from chemic dissolution springs,
And gives to matter its eccentric wings;
With strong Repulsion parts the exploding mass,
Melts into lymph, or kindles into gas.
Attraction next, as earth or air subsides,
The ponderous atoms from the light divides,
Approaching parts with quick embrace combines.
Swells into spheres, and lengthens into lines.
Last, as fine goads the gluten-threads excits,
Cords grapple cords, and webs with webs units;
And quick Contraction with ethereal flame
Lights into life the fibre-woven frame.
Hence without parent by spontaneous birth
Rise the first specks of animated earth;
From Nature's womb the plant or insect swims,
And buds or breathes, with microscopic limbs.[23]

In his theory on meter, therefore, as well as in choice of the traditional meter in which to write, Darwin demonstrates his respect for abstract artifice. On the other hand, his variations in this meter approach the less artificial strong-stress metrics of the end of the century.

III

In addition to meter, Darwin uses many other devices of rhetorical figures and sound patterns to thicken the language of his verse. The heroic couplet originated in English at a time when the figures of rhetoric were well known and respected, and it grew to maturity and flourished in the century when Renaissance rhetorics were used as composition textbooks for schoolboys.[24] Wimsatt says that the best explanation of the

[23] Darwin, *The Temple of Nature*, canto I, 11. 233-250.
[24] For the origin of the couplet, see Ruth Wallerstein, "The Development of the Rhetoric and Metre of the Heroic Couplet, Especially in 1625-1645" in Bernard Schilling, ed., *Essential Articles for the Study of English Augustan Backgrounds* (Hamden: Archon, 1961). For the simultaneous interest in the figures, see Sister

figures of speech and thought in Pope's couplets is George Puttenham's *Arte of English Poesie* (1589), and he assumed that "these perhaps had been learned so well by Pope as a boy that he could forget them," since Pope does not mention the figures in his correspondence or criticism.[25] Darwin undoubtedly received a similar training at Chesterfield School in the rhetorical figures as principles of composition. A letter written by Darwin at the age of sixteen to his sister Susannah shows the schoolboy interest at that time in language devices:

... was I to give you a journal of a Week, it would be stuft [sic.] so full of Greek and Latin as translation, verses, themes annotation Exercises and ye like it would not only be very tedious and insipid but perfectly unintelligible to any but Schoolboys.[26]

The spirits of Puttenham and his popularizers were to haunt the Botanic Garden just as they do Windsor Forest.

Ruth Wallerstein's historical account of the development of the closed couplet stanza correlates well with Sister Miriam Joseph's account of the popularity of figurist rhetoric to show the mutual influence of the two developments on each other. The popularity of the rhetorical theory undoubtedly encouraged the use of the couplet, just as the existence of good couplet verse was a justification of the rhetoric. Independent of the historical argument for the simultaneous development of the couplet verse pattern and of the figurist theory of rhetoric, students of the details of poetic language have also noticed that the fully developed couplet is particularly suited to the use of certain figures of speech. Geoffrey Tillotson noticed this characteristic of the couplet in a study that did not include any reference to figurist rhetoric, but dealt with other matters. He writes:

Within particular couplets the poet worked out as many contrasts and parallels as he could, providing the maximum number of internal geometrical relationships ... in Pope a couplet will often suggest a figure in Euclid. ... [It] is a metre for educated people. No meaning is possible for the "mind" to review, or for the "spirit" to kindle at, till the "brain" has mastered the Euclidean relationships.[27]

Miriam Joseph's discussion of the difference between the figurists, the traditionalists, and the Ramists in the English Renaissance. Briefly, the figurists, among whom the most famous was Puttenham, were in favor of teaching only elocution, one of the five parts of rhetoric. Elocution dealt only with the figures of speech. But actually the figurists included all the other parts of rhetoric, such as invention, as figures of speech. Sister Miriam Joseph, pp. 13ff.

[25] Wimsatt, *The Verbal Icon*, pp. 175-76.
[26] Quoted in Charles Darwin, preliminary notice to Ernst Krause, *Erasmus Darwin* (London, 1879), p. 10.
[27] Geoffrey Tillotson, *Augustan Poetic Diction* (London: University of London, 1964), pp. 14-15.

Jacob Adler noticed the suitability of the couplet to particular rhetorical figures in his study of the prosody of Pope. The metrical balance of the two-line stanza, which is augmented by the tendency toward medical caesura, makes the couplet a perfect envelope for statements involving parallelism and repetition; and Adler demonstrates that Pope's couplets abound in the figures of rhetorical repetition: anaphora, antithesis, zeugma, and chiasmus.[28]

Examples of all of these figures can be found in Darwin's verse. He especially seems to be fond of chiasmus.[29] Similarly, the artful repetition of word patterns is a principle of organization for the sentence and the paragraph in Darwin's verse although there is no one name for this as a schematic figure of speech.[30] Repetition and variation of the basic sentence pattern of adjective, noun, verb, adjective, noun, which fits so nicely into the pentameter line with medial caesura, is a device for achieving thickness as well as unity in small sections. The verse paragraphs in the first canto of "The Loves of the Plants" are shorter than in any other canto of the three poems and in several of them Darwin uses this principle of organization skillfully. The result is a series of highly figured, short paragraphs – little cameos. Darwin himself gives the best description of those short paragraphs in the "Proem" to this poem, and the description is characteristic of his laughing, self-demeaning tone. He says they should be contemplated "as diverse little pictures suspended over the chimney of a lady's dressing room, *connected only by a slight festoon of ribbons.*" [31]

If the connections between the little pictures in Darwin's verse is slight, their internal verbal structure often is not. One of the more intricate examples is the following:

> a   n   a   n   v
> With vain desire the pensive Alcea burns,
> a   n   v   v
> And, like sad Eloisa, loves and mourns.
> a   n   v   a   n
> The freckled Iris owns a fiercer flame,

[28] Jacob Adler, *The Reach of Art, A Study in the Prosody of Pope* (Gainsville: Univ. of Florida, 1964), pp. 12-17.

[29] See my doctoral dissertation *The Poems of Erasmus Darwin*, Diss. Columbia Univ. 1967.

[30] Adler describes the numerous kinds of rhetorical balance and repetition for which there are no names: "Beyond zeugma, chiasmus, anaphora, and antithesis, balancing of phrase with phrase, clause with clause, hemistich with hemistich, line with line, couplet with couplet: and artful repetition of word or of word arrangement in a never-ending variety. . . ." Adler, p. 20.

[31] Darwin, *The Botanic Garden*, Part II, p. xvi.

a a n v n
And *three* unjealous husbands wed the dame.
n a v a n
Cupressus dark disdains his dusky bride,
a n v a n v
One dome contains them, but two beds divide.
a n v a n
The proud Osyris flees his angry fair,
a n v a n
Two houses hold the fashionable pair.[13]

Each plant has a different, though related, sexual problem; and each couplet has a different, though related, word pattern. The sexual activity varies from complete impotency in the case of *Alcea,* where some plants have no stamens, to two varieties of vigorous marital activity. The fourth case, *Cupressus,* is personified as a marriage, but with very little sex. The most interesting feature in the paragraph is the variation in the basic pattern of one verb per line surrounded by substantives and adjectives. I think that this is the "healthy" pattern, for it is nearly repeated in the two couplets describing active sex. In the couplets devoted to *Alcea* and *Cupressus,* however, this pattern breaks down. Perhaps Darwin is associating the grace and balance of the basic pattern with fulfillment whereas the lack of pattern is associated with lack of fulfillment. In any case, the paragraph is a nicely figured collection of patterned word units and naughty subject matter.

Such a paragraph, however, is not typical of the majority of Darwin's verses because he prefers longer paragraphs with more development. One of his favorite devices for development is the long digression, much like the Homeric simile. He loves to tell stories of lovers, either from mythology or from recent history, as illustrations in his description of natural objects. For instance, he tells the story of Proserpine being seized by Pluto to illustrate a chemical reaction of Priestley's; he tells the story of the rape of Europa to illustrate another natural process; he tells a story from recent history of a young couple burned to death on their wedding night as part of an exhortation to the element water to extinguish fires. All of these stories are more elaborated than the brief references to Eloise and Abelard above. Many of them are quite well-told little stories, and many of them deal with sex. A good example is the long digression Darwin uses to illustrate the chemical reaction of nitrogen and oxygen. During the course of this reaction a reddish vapor is given off and heat escapes. Darwin compared this to Mars' seduction of Venus and Vulcan's ensuing anger, which ties the "illicit lovers" together with

[32] Darwin, "The Loves of the Plants," canto I, 11. 69-76.

a net, that is, the chemical bond. It is a good story, which Darwin tells well, and a good example of the long digression as a rhetorical device:

> So Beauty's Goddess, warm with new desire,
> Left, on her silver wheels, the God of Fire;
> Her faithless charms to fiercer Mars resign'd,
> Met with fond lips, with wanton arms intwin'd.
> – Indignant Vulcan eyed the parting Fair,
> And watch'd with jealous step the guilty pair;
> O'er his broad neck a wiry net he flung,
> Quick as he strode, the tinkling meshes rung;
> Fine as the spider's flimsy thread He wove
> The immortal toil to lime illicit love;
> Steel were the knots, and steel the twisted thong,
> Ring link'd in ring, indissolubly strong;
> On viewless hooks along the fretted roof
> He hung, unseen, the inextricable woof. –
> – Quick start the springs, the webs pellucid spread,
> And lock the embracing Lovers on their bed;
> Fierce with loud taunts vindictive Vulcan springs
> Tries all the bolts, and tightens all the strings,
> Shakes with incessant shouts the bright abodes,
> Claps his rude hands, and calls the festive Gods. –
> – With spreading palms the alarmed Goddess tries
> To veil her beauties from celestial eyes,
> Writhes her fair limbs, the slender ringlets strains,
> And bids her Loves untie the obdurate chains;
> Soft swells her panting bosom, as she turns,
> And her flush'd cheek with brighter blushes burns.
> Majestic grief the Queen of Heaven avows,
> And chaste Minerva hides her helmed brows;
> Attendant Nymphs with bashful eyes askance
> Steal of intangled Mars a transient glance;
> Surrounding Gods the circling nectar quaff,
> Gaze on the Fair, and envy as they laugh.[33]

IV

Smaller details such as sound resemblances and rhyme often provide opportunities for interesting thickening. Sometimes the sound resemblance

---

[33] Darwin, "The Economy of Vegetation," canto II, 11 151-82.

of a verb and its object can be used to underline a very funny image, and to suggest a metaphoric rhyme that is so incongruous that the reader laughs. In most cases, I think that Darwin is creating these humorous effects intentionally in order to maintain the comic tone although it is possible that in some places he simply gets carried away with visual imagery and with rhyme and that the incongruity is unintentional. In a description of St. Cecilia singing, he takes the common image of the snow-white bosom of a female and the image of pearly-white teeth and animates them so that St. Cecilia becomes a kind of singing snow machine:

> [make] . . . her bosom's rising snow,
> O'er her white teeth in tuneful accents flow.[34]

The noun-verb rhyme punctuates the image and makes it seem metaphorically fitting that a singer with a snow-white bosom should inevitably have white teeth. The comic tone in Darwin's verse does often derive from his treating small or insignificant objects in the grand manner, that is from the traditional mock-heroic technique. One device that he uses to underline the incongruity between the small and the grand is the verb-noun rhyme. In the following example, the verb refers to a grand action, the swinging shut of a dungeon portal, whereas the noun refers to a very small object indeed. Notice also how the placing of both the caesura and the enjambement in the first line create a long cadence in the second line, which supports the grand tone applied to a small object:

> So sleeps in silence the Curculio, shut
> In the dark chambers of the cavern'd nut.[35]

In addition to creating a more or less comic tone (not as funny, I think, as the snow machine), the rhyme in this example has an important metaphoric function. A shut nut is literally a very large cavern from the point of view of the Curculio, or weevil; and the rhyme makes the image seem more appropriate.

Feminine rhyme, the traditional rhyme device for comic effects, is used very sparingly by Darwin and never with the sure comic clinching effect of Byron. In the following two couplets, the comic tone is primarily a result of the exaggerated personification; but the rhymes, which are almost feminine in both couplets, help:

---

[34] *Ibid.*, canto IV, 11. 249-50.
[35] Darwin, "The Loves of the Plants," canto IV, 11. 431-32.

> – Hither, emerging from yon orient skies,
> Botanic Goddess! bend thy radiant eyes.[36]
> As woos Azotic Gas the virgin Air,
> And veils in crimson clouds the yielding Fair.[37]

The chance sound resemblances here also approach metaphor. The bending eyes of the Goddess are associated with the rays of the sun rising in the east, just as both of the rhyming epithets in the second couplet refer to oxygen.

This primitive yet highly artificial level of meaning whereby a similarity is suggested that has no logical explanation except a chance sound resemblance is probably seen in its most extreme form in the pun, a close cousin of rhyme. When Hamlet says he is too much in the sun, the pun adds metaphoric levels of meaning to the statement that derive from the pure accident that sun and son sound alike in English. Similarly, in the following couplet from Darwin's verse, the rhyme of "bear" and "Bear" is a verb-object rhyme; but the pun creates the effect of two nouns. Thus the "fiend of frost" who is being exiled by the Botanic Goddess is not only taken to and chained to the "Northern Bear," but also becomes a "Tyrant bear" himself:

> To Zembla's moon-bright coast the Tyrant bear,
> And chain him howling to the Northern Bear.[38]

(Darwin's poems remind me of the works of Vladimir Nabokov in many ways: the extreme artificiality, the long notes, the ribald sex, the comic tone, and here the passing reference to Zembla, an important locality for Nabokov.)

Another familiar sound pattern, consonant alliteration, seldom augments the meaning, but is generally used simply to reinforce the effect of the stated meaning; and thus it is much closer, as a rhetorical device, to the representative meter mentioned above than to metaphoric rhyme. Following are four couplets with considerable consonant patterning in each of them, most of it alliteration:

> Shrill scream the famish'd bats, and shivering owls,
> And loud and long the dog of midnight howls! [39]
> O'er the green floor, and round the dew-damp wall,

---

[36] Darwin, "The Economy of Vegetation," canto I, 11. 43-44.
[37] *Ibid.*, canto II, 11. 147-48.
[38] *Ibid.*, canto I, 11. 441-42.
[39] Darwin, "The Loves of the Plants," canto III, 11. 13-14.

> The slimy snail, and bloated lizard crawl.[40]
> Dread scenes of Death, in nodding sables dress'd,
> Froze the broad eye, and thrill'd the unbreathing breast.[41]
> Each shifting scene, some patriot hero trod,
> Some sainted beauty, or some savious god.[42]

In the first two examples, the appropriateness of the repeated consonant sounds to the "screaming" and the "crawling" respectively seems particularly representative. Also, the contrast in the first couplet between the "screaming" and the vowel patterning for the "howling" is effective.

Anna Seward thought that Darwin used too much alliteration, and a look at the examples quoted in this chapter will show that he does frequently use alliteration to link words in a line and to bind an adjective more closely to its noun. Miss Seward writes:

[alliteration] often increases, and sometimes entirely constitutes, that power which, by a metaphoric expression... is called *picturesque sound*... it's [sic.] too frequent use in a poem, or too lavish repetition in a single line or couplet, will injure what it is designed to improve.[43]

Although Miss Seward does not cite either of the two following couplets, they would probably have come under her censure.[44] I think that in both cases, however, the alliteration reinforces the stated meaning effectively; and also the rhyme in both examples is metaphoric, although not of the extreme, most interesting, kind that brings together distantly related objects. The two couplets create nearly opposite effects. The first is brash and phantasmagoric, like the Miltonic hell it echoes:

> So on his Nightmare through the evening fog
> Flits the squab Fiend o'er fen, and lake, and bog.[45]

The second is more quiet and Keatsian:

> Pomona's hand replenish'd Plenty's horn,
> And Ceres laugh'd amid her seas of corn.[46]

[40] Darwin, *The Temple of Nature*, canto I, 11. 119-20.
[41] *Ibid.*, canto I, 11. 143-144.
[42] *Ibid.*, canto I, 11. 153-54.
[43] Seward, pp. 308-09.
[44] The line she does mention after the above quotation is not, I think, as ineffective as Miss Seward thinks:
> Again the Goddess strikes her golden lyre,
> And tunes to wilder note the warbling wire.
I do think, however, that the rhyme is unfortunate here and may have been caused by the desire to alliterate. "The Loves of the Plants," canto II, 11. 1-2.
[45] *Ibid.*, canto III, 11. 51-52. See *Paradise Lost*, II, 11. 614-28.
[46] Darwin, *The Temple of Nature*, canto I, 11. 407-408.

In fact, later in the same poem there is a line that may have suggested to Keats his line 242 in *The Eve of St. Agnes* ("Blinded alike from sunshine and from rain"), another skillful creation of sensuousness by Darwin:

> Web within web involves his larva form
> Alike secured from sunshine and from storm.[47]

Finally, all these verse techniques are part of the general gaudiness of Darwin's poetry which is usually visual. A common objection to Darwin's accumulation of verbal and visual detail is that there is simply too much detail; his descriptions are too rich. Geoffrey Tillotson has an answer to this charge:

... if Darwin is gaudy, he is not inane. Nor is the gaudiness wanton, for it is that of bits and pieces of the natural world itself. Darwin is a scientist who writes accurately.[48]

Tillotson then chooses for illustration a passage from Darwin's verse that is a description not of botany, but of geology. It is a catalogue of personified metals full of descriptive epithets that are accurate while at the same time exotic and colorful. Tillotson calls one (living silver) "an excellent item of diction" for historical reasons.[49] But the most striking characteristic of the verse is simply its heavy texture. I quote a few more lines than Tillotson in order to give a final example of an eighteen-line passage as thick in visual detail and exotic vocabulary, I believe, as much in Keats or Spenser, for example. The Botanic Goddess speaks to the "element" earth:

> "Gnomes! you then taught volcanic airs to force
> Through bubbling Lavas their resistless course,
> O'er the broad walls of rifted Granite climb,
> And pierce the rent roof of incumbent Lime,
> Round sparry caves metallic lustres fling,
> And bear phlogiston on their tepid wing.
>   "Hence glows [sic.] refulgent Tin! thy crystal grains,
> And tawny Copper shoots her azure veins;
> Zinc lines his fretted vault with sable ore,
> And dull Galena tessellates the floor;

---

[47] *Ibid.,* canto II, 11. 299-300.
[48] Tillotson, pp. 93-94. See also p. 24.
[49] Tillotson writes, *"Living silver* is an excellent item of diction, framed by analogy from Virgil's phrase for statuary *spiranta aera (Aeneid,* vi. 847). Pliny's name for mercury, *vivum argentum,* lacks the engaging present participle." *Ibid.,* p. 94n.

On vermil beds in Idria's mighty caves
The living Silver rolls its ponderous waves;
With gay refractions bright Platina shines,
And studs with squander'd stars his dusky mines;
Long threads of netted gold, and silvery darts,
Inlay the Lazuli, and pierce the Quartz; –
– Whence roof'd with silver beam'd Peru, of old,
And hapless Mexico was paved with gold.[50]

V

None of the technical devices described in this chapter, except perhaps the overall visualism and gaudiness of texture mentioned last, was really new in Darwin's century. The heroic couplet, in particular, (even though Darwin writes very skillful couplets) has a tendency of seeming too automatically mechanical and not artificial and varied enough. Truly lively, imaginative motion, in other words, which Darwin theorized well about, is often lacking in the details of his poetic practice. Darwin adopted, and in fact used skillfully, too many pat rhetorical devices for thickening his verse. He did not break enough new ground with his verse and his language invention although his theory on artificiality suggests that he should have. He is no Gerard Manley Hopkins in the details of language invention. This is also the conclusion of James V. Logan, the only other 20th-century critic to look closely at the details of Darwin's verse: "He was not enough of a genius or let us at least say he was not original enough, to evolve a new style based on his own healthy theory." [51] Ironically, then, in the technical areas of language invention, although he is interestingly "strange" to some extent, Darwin failed by not giving imaginative motion enough free rein, by being too "strict" in his analogies.

[50] Darwin, "The Economy of Vegetation," canto II, ll. 395-412.
[51] Logan, p. 84.

CHAPTER FIVE

THE FULL COMEDIAN: A FINAL LOOSE ANALOGY

Jovial Crispin, in calamitous crape?
... For realists, what is is what should be.

Wallace Stevens,
"The Comedian as the Letter C"

I

In addition to a healthy theory, what does not fail in Darwin's writing is the sense of overall tone and a few larger cameo pieces. Several longer passages of his verse have already been quoted and discussed in earlier chapters. These have been little anecdotes or stories that have some self-contained unity. I will deal with two more in this final chapter – longer passages and more unified. Strangely enough, Desmond King-Hele who has edited the only collection of Darwin's writings in this century apparently does not think that there are sustained passages of unified writing in the poems, and so he only anthologizes little snippets of verse.[1] The longer passages ought to be seen, I think, for what they are – memorable sections in admittedly weakly unified poems.

Actually, at least two recent writers have taken Darwin's poems even more seriously than this. They have not anthologized nor even tried to explain particular couplets very closely, but they have sought to explain a working unity of theme and subject matter throughout the entire poetic output of "The Loves of the Plants," "The Economy of Vegetation," and *The Temple of Nature*. Elizabeth Sewell has included Darwin's poems in very exalted company indeed in her recent discussion of the tradition that she calls Orphism.[2] This tradition, as she describes it, includes writers and scientists who have made use of the Orpheus myth, from Ovid and Shakespeare to lesser known figures such as Linnaeus. But more basically, according to Miss Sewell, this tradition is concerned with the purpose underlying all scientific investigation, and it produces

---

[1] Desmond King-Hele, ed., *The Essential Writings of Erasmus Darwin* (London: MacGibbon & Kee, 1968).
[2] Elizabeth Sewell, *The Orphic Voice* (London: Routledge & Kegan Paul, 1960).

a particular class of writing. In Orphic works, scientific knowledge goes hand in hand with rhetoric and poetry. When Miss Sewell describes the gradual accumulation of biological data in the 18th century, which eventually suggested the theory of evolution to Darwin and to others, it is clear that Darwin's science does not seem at odds with his poetry to her. She writes:

Classification and description of living beings, accompanied by the inquiries, which are bound to follow, into relationships in time as well as space [that is, detailed biological classification showing difference at any given time would logically suggest evolution through time] – these are the classic achievements of the seventeenth and eighteenth centuries in natural science, culminating in Linnaeus who is of the Orphic line himself. ... It is not surprising, then, that at this point ... the respective Orpheus figures of Erasmus Darwin and Goethe appear, at the point of the recognition and appraisal of natural forms and the application of words to them.[3]

Darwin's decision and ability, therefore, to versify the sexual, botanical classification system of Linnaeus would seem to associate his poems, according to Miss Sewell, with the Orphic tradition.

Also, Miss Sewell includes myth as an important ingredient of the Orphic tradition, and thus takes Darwin's mythological machinery and pictorial use of imagery very seriously, as we discussed in the chapter on his visualism. Irwin Primer, writing most recently in a favorable way about Darwin's poems, agrees with Miss Sewell and has added to her interpretation of Darwin by pointing out that there is a primitivistic or non-progressive theme inherent in Darwin's science and expressed in his poetry and that this theme gives at least his final poem a solid, meaningful unity. Primer writes:

His poem [*The Temple of Nature*, which both Miss Sewell and Primer think is his best] and his world-view depend on the mutual support which scientific progress and pagan myths can give to each other ... the strongest primitivistic strain in Darwin's thought is his proclivity toward myth – his willingness to believe that the Egyptian priests had arrived at the basic truths of Nature, that these truths became known in Greece and were taught in the Eleusinian Mysteries, and they survive embedded in the pagan myths. Hence, for Darwin, the progress of knowledge is in some sense also a recovery of lost wisdom.[4]

One other feature of Darwin's poems interests Miss Sewell in particular and helps to create the unity of meaning she finds in them. This is the

---

[3] *Ibid.*, p. 172.
[4] Irwin Primer, "Erasmus Darwin's *Temple of Nature*: Progress, Evolution and the Eleusinian Mysteries," in *Journal of the History of Ideas*, 25 (January-March 1964), 63-64.

comic love-marriage motif, which is most apparent in "The Loves of the Plants" but which appears continually in the other poems as well. Miss Sewell interprets this preoccupation with the theme of sex as another agreement of Darwin with the Orphic tradition:

> It is this [plant sexuality] in Linnaeus which Darwin primarily celebrates, moving on from there to celebrate sex itself in *Phytologia* [a prose treatise much like the *Zoonomia*, but shorter, on plant life] as "the chef d'oeuvre," the masterpiece of nature. [This is also the theme of canto II of *The Temple of Nature*]
> The Orphic mind is active at this point, and we begin to see what lies behind the shift in our prevailing Orpheus figure from that of the ordering of nature to that of the search for Eurydice.[5]

Although I admire and am initially sympathetic to these efforts to find unified mythic meaning in Darwin's writing, I think Miss Sewell fails to emphasize the one aspect of the Orpheus myth that seems most relevant to Darwin: its indeterminacy, the impossibility of any complete and final consummation for Orpheus. Thus I feel that neither she nor Primer completely understands Darwin's comic vision. It is implicit in the story of Orpheus that love and marriage cannot achieve the union that human beings would like. The comic vision expresses full awareness of this limitation and attempts to make the best of it. In fact, I think the most important part of the overall effect of Darwin's poems is the communication of skepticism. The poems are "scientific" in the sense that they do not provide any unified mythic meaning. What they celebrate is motion and indeterminacy, and because of this they are nervous in tone. They also celebrate imaginative motion, man's way to make life less "vapid," but, as we concluded in the previous chapter, without allowing enough inventive free rein. Thus they fail to invent the "supreme fiction" of imaginative motion, and they certainly do not reveal supreme truth – except in the indeterminate sense of matter in motion.

II

The two most sparkling longer cameos, or scenical representations, in my opinion, appear in "The Economy of Vegetation," the first part of *The Botanic Garden* that Darwin hesitantly published second. If one takes his large mythic meaning seriously, as Miss Sewell and Primer do, then *The Temple of Nature* is seen as the culmination of his vision; but I tend to agree here not with the literary critics but with the scientific historian of the Lunar Society, Robert Schofield, who says that Darwin's

---

[5] Sewell, p. 209.

last poem is a "tired book [with] little of the verbal polish and brilliant imagery which help excuse the poetic defects of the *Botanic Garden*." [6] I would argue that it is fruitless to try to rehabilitate Darwin the scientific theorist, who tries rather unsuccessfully to use imaginative motion, as a mythic poet. He should be appreciated for what he is: an original thinker caught in a particularly modern dilemma. In any case, there are two longish passages in the earlier poem that are worth quoting in their entirety in order to see Darwin's strange, precious imaginative motion with the comic tone at its best.

Not sure of myth, too analytic to accept the illusions of imaginative motion as anything other than what they are, Darwin nevertheless keeps wanting to mingle anthropocentric phenomena like love with what he knows of physical motion in the environment. To personify natural processes in this way becomes, I think, for Darwin consciously tense and consciously humorous. He knows a lot about motions in nature, such as the weather, and he knows a lot about human or "animal" motion. But they seem very distant, very theoretical in fact. Apparently he concludes that the only solution is to face these absurd, non-anthropocentric motions directly, to personify them, to try to make them visual. One result is to show us how alone we are in our imaginative motions, and yet how similar these motions are to all motion in the universe. All motion curves alone, and the communion is in this aloneness. If this is what the mythic meaning of eternal return that Primer mentions points to, then there is mythic meaning in Darwin. But it is pretty barren as simple curving motion, and it makes Darwin shudder with laughter.

One of the most successful shuddering little personifications of this kind is the story of Juno's enticement or recepture of the affections of her flirtatious husband, Jupiter, which allegorizes the chemical reaction of oxygen and hydrogen to form water. Scientific opinion of Darwin's time apparently held that such a reaction was partially responsible for rain, so that the following story is a personification not only of chemical phenomena but also of meteorological. As is typical of his organization in most of these little stories, Darwin first gives a personified description of the physical event and then moves into an extended allegorical simile. I also quote the relevant note at the end to give the whole cameo:

"NYMPHS! YOUR bright squadrons watch with chemic eyes
The cold-elastic vapours, as they rise;

[6] Robert E. Schofield, *The Lunar Society of Birmingham* (Oxford: Oxford Univ. Press, 1963), p. 402. Bernard Blackstone also agrees with this judgment of *The Temple of Nature*. See *The Consecrated Urn* (London: Longmans Green, 1959), p. 8.

With playful force arrest them as they pass,
And to *pure* AIR betroth the *flaming* GAS.
Round their translucent forms at once they fling
Their rapturous arms, with silver bosoms cling;
In fleecy clouds their fluttering wings extend,
Or from the skies in lucid showers descend;
Whence rills and rivers owe their secret birth,
And Ocean's hundred arms infold the earth.
"So, robed by Beauty's Queen, with softer charms
SATURNIA woo'd the Thunderer to her arms;
O'er her fair limbs a veil of light she spread,
And bound a starry diadem on her head;
Long braids of pearl her golden tresses grac'd,
And the charm'd CESTUS sparkled round her waist.
– Raised o'er the woof, by Beauty's hand inwrought,
Breathes the soft Sigh, and glows the enamour'd Thought;
Vows on light wings succeed, and quiver'd Wiles,
Assuasive Accents, and seductive Smiles.
– Slow rolls the Cyprian car in purple pride,
And, steer'd by LOVE, ascends admiring Ide;
Climbs the green slopes, the nodding woods pervades,
Burns round the rocks, or gleams amid the shades. –
Glad ZEPHYR leads the train, and waves above
The barbed darts, and blazing torch of Love;
Reverts his smiling face, and pausing flings
Soft showers of roses from aurelian wings.
Delighted Fawns, in wreathes of flowers array'd,
With tiptoe Wood-Boys beat the chequer'd glade;
Alarmed Naiads, rising into air,
Lift o'er their silver urns their leafy hair;
Each to her oak the bashful Dryads shrink,
And azure eyes are seen through every chink.
– LOVE culls a flaming shaft of broadest wing,
And rests the fork upon the quivering string;
Points his arch eye aloft, with fingers strong
Draws to his curled ear the silken thong;
Loud twangs the steel, the golden arrow flies,
Trails a long line of lustre through the skies;
"'Tis done!" he shouts, "the mighty Monarch feels!"
And with loud laughter shakes the silver wheels;
Bends o'er the car, and whirling, as it moves,

His loosen'd bowstring, drives the rising doves.
– Pierced on his throne the starting Thunderer turns,
Melts with soft sighs, with kindling rapture burns;
Clasps her fair hand, and eyes in fond amaze
The bright Intruder with enamour'd gaze.
"And leaves my Goddess, like a blooming bride,
"The fanes of Argos for the rocks of Ide?
"Her gorgeous palaces, and amaranth bowers,
"For cliff-top'd mountains, and aerial towers?"
He said; and, leading from her ivory seat
The blushing Beauty to his lone retreat,
Curtain'd with night the couch imperial shrouds,
And rests the crimson cushions upon clouds. –
Earth feels the grateful influence from above,
Sighs the soft Air, and Ocean murmurs love;
Etherial Warmth expands his brooding wing,
And in still showers descends the genial Spring.

And in still showers. 1. 260. The allegorical interpretation of the very antient mythology which supposes Jupiter to represent the superior part of the atmosphere or ether, and Juno the inferior air, and that the conjunction of these two produced vernal showers, as alluded to in Virgil's Georgics, is so analogous to the present important discovery of the production of water from pure air, or oxygene, and inflammable air, or hydrogen, (which from its greater levity probably resides over the former,) that one should be tempted to believe that the very antient chemists of Egypt had discovered the composition of water, and thus represented it in their hieroglyphic figures before the invention of letters.[7]

The key image here, which is reinforced by the frequent use of the figure of chiasmus or reverse parallelism, is the image of cyclical patterns or circularity which is so important in a description of the water cycle. Not only is there vertical circularity in the fact of water going up and coming down, but also there is horizontal circularity suggested when the Botanic Goddess notices that the oceans "infold the earth." In fact, the whole passage to me resembles Shelley's description of the water cycle in "The Cloud" with one major difference: Shelley's poem is more subtle in its serious metaphysical imagery while Darwin's broad allegory has a more burlesque and daring effect of tone. The chemical and meteorological reaction allegorized by Juno and Jupiter is erotic and thus strong (like that liaison of Venus and Mars quoted earlier), and this is a good simile for the turbulence of the sky. The image is also rather

---

[7] Erasmus Darwin, *The Botanic Garden, Part I* (London: J. Johnson, 1791), "The Economy of Vegetation," canto III, 11. 201-260 and pp. 136-37n.

funny in the sly way that Darwin hints that the rain may be associated
with the resulting sexual orgasm. Darwin's understanding of the cycles
and forces in nature is profound, and at the same time detached. He
knows that all things are analogous, which makes human love little more
than a meteorological phenomenon of motion. He is the comic poet and
philosopher, like Byron, believing and yet fearing to believe in the non-
anthropocentric unity that he sees.

If there are recurring themes in Darwin's poems, they are all related
to one prime interest: birth, or possibly continually renewing motion.
In a sense, this is the theme of the cycles that Primer mentions – but
very barren, non-anthropocentric cycles. There is an alliterative phrase
that Darwin likes well enough to repeat several times that refers to sexual
birth, regeneration, and cycling metamorphosis all at once. The phrase
is "buds or breathes." It appears slightly modified in a prose "Interlude"
of "The Loves of the Plants"; it appears in *The Temple of Nature*; it
also appears at the end of the most effective passage of "The Economy
of Vegetation" near the end of Canto IV:

> "SYLPHS! as you hover on ethereal wing,
> Brood the green children of parturient Spring! –
> Where in their burstling cells my Embryons rest,
> I charge you guard the vegetable nest;
> Count with nice eye the myriad SEEDS, that swell
> Each vaulted womb of husk, or pod, or shell;
> Feed with sweet juices, cloths with downy hair,
> Or hang, inshrined, their little orbs in air.
>   "So, late decry'd by HERSCHEL's piercing sight,
> Hang the bright squadrons of the twinkling Night;
> Ten thousand marshall'd stars, a silver zone,
> Effuse their blended lustres round her throne;
> Suns call to suns, in lucid clouds conspire,
> And light exterior skies with golden fire;
> Resistless rolls the illimitable sphere,
> And one great circle forms the unmeasured year.
> – Roll on, YE STARS! exult in youthful prime,
> Mark with bright curves the printless steps of Time;
> Near and more near your beamy cars approach,
> And lessening orbs on lessening orbs encroach; –
> Flowers of the sky! ye too to age must yield,
> Frail as your silken sisters of the field!
> Star after star from Heaven's high arch shall rush,

Suns sink on suns, and systems systems crush,
Headlong, extinct, to one dark centre fall,
And Death and Night and Chaos mingle all!
– Till o'er the wreck, emerging from the storm,
Immortal NATURE lifts her changeful form,
Mounts from her funeral pyre on wings of flame,
And soars and shines, another and the same.
    2. "Lo! on each SEED within its slender rind
Life's golden threads in endless circles wind;
Maze within maze the lucid webs are roll'd,
And, as they burst, the living flame unfold.
The Pulpy acorn, ere it swells, contains
The Oak's vast branches in its milky veins;
Each ravel's bud, fine film, and fibre-line
Traced with nice pencil on the small design.
The young Narcissus, in it's bulb compress'd,
Cradles a second nestling on its breast;
In whose fine arms a younger embryon lies,
Folds its thin leaves, and shuts its floret-eyes;
Grain within grain successive harvests dwell,
And boundless forests slumber in a shell.
– So yon grey precipice, and ivy'd towers,
Long winding meads, and intermingled bowers,
Green files of poplars, o'er the lake that bow,
And glimmering wheel, which rolls and foams below,
In one bright point with nice distinction lie
Plan'd on the moving tablet of the eye.
– So, fold on fold, Earth's wavy plains extend,
And, sphere on sphere, its hidden strate bend; –
Incumbent Spring her beamy plumes expands
O'er restless oceans, and impatient lands,
With genial lustres warms the mighty ball,
And the GREAT SEED evolves, disclosing ALL;
LIFE *buds or breathes* from Indus to the Poles,
And the vast surface kindles, as it rolls! [8]

The passage is a lyric celebration of birth: astronomical birth, plant birth, animal birth, geological birth, and, in the lines on a picturesque sketch or painting, artistic or imaginative birth. The predominant image in the passage is the image of the first great egg of night from which "Divine

---

[8] *Ibid.,* canto IV, 11. 351-408.

Love" produced the universe. This is a myth, of course, but it is a peculiarly non-anthropocentric myth expressing little more than continual, circling motion. Darwin had alluded to this myth early in Canto I of "The Economy of Vegetation" in the passage on the creation of the heavens that Walpole liked so much (quoted in chapter three above). Here at the end of the poem, he puts together a beautifully intricate development of the idea.[9] The image of the egg itself suggests circularity, or the curve of beauty, and Darwin emphasizes this shape by noticing circularity first in tiny seeds, then in solar systems, then in seeds again, then in the human eye, and finally in terrestrial geography for picturesque art. Everything is round and spinning: a figure both for continual regeneration and for meaningless spiraling. The passage is my favorite piece of Darwinian verse, and it celebrates continual circling motion.

III

At the beginning of this book I invoked three 18th-century writers to help illuminate Darwin's dilemma and despair. But actually Darwin is closer in spirit, if not in final accomplishment, to later celebrants of the power of imaginative motion in the face of meaningless despair. In particular, Darwin's celebration of curving ripeness, his singing in the sun, suggests to me the poetic stance and even some of the passages of Wallace Stevens. And I can think of no better way to end this discussion of Darwin's attitudes toward and uses of imaginative motion than to suggest one final loose analogy.

Wallace Stevens, the "portly Azcan" of his bumptious little poem "Bantams in Pine-Woods," was apparently another robust materialist. Like Hume, "le bon David," and like Darwin he was large in stature and large in his ability to enjoy life. Also, like them, he had a well sharpened sense of irony in order to defend his inherent love of life and desire to "trust nature" against the vision of meaningless random motion that forces itself upon modern man. Stevens also was sensitive to the burden of the past, to the competition and largeness of human culture, as one corner of the chaos of random motion; and his writings are laced throughout with nervous reticence about his own poetic ambition that reminds me of Darwin's comic irony on the same topic. Even though Stevens' reputation is very high right now, he himself developed a whole rationale and wrote often about accepting the role of minor poet. "The Comedian as the Letter C," which reminds me most of Darwin and which is largely auto-

---

[9] See *Ibid.*, canto I, 11. 97ff.

biographical, is about being a minor poet. Stevens himself was safely successful in a non-literary career of law and business as Darwin made a small fortune from his medical practice. Although he was a promising student-poet like Darwin, Stevens also delayed the serious pursuit of a literary reputation until middle life. In other words, there is every indication that Stevens had no illusions about the "divine gift" of the poet at the same time that his skepticism was all embracing enough to convince him that the self-reliant imaginative motion of the individual was the only source of meaning, and that no meaning at all.[10] This "religion" of imaginative motion was eloquently expressed for us by Stevens, and our imaginative knowledge and sense of one of the little known precursors of it will be helped by looking at a few of Stevens' words.

The full acceptance of meaninglessness and of man's responsibility to be self-reliant in the face of it has always been too shocking to take straight. It has required either the sugar-coating of illusion or the detachment of irony. The humor of Hume and Darwin's polite playing with and mockery of his reader are both early ancestors in tone of Stevens' brilliant and playful blast:

> Poetry is the supreme fiction, madame. . . .
> This will make widows wince. But fictive things
> Wink as they will. Wink most when widows wince.[11]

The wincing and the winking are the physiological activities that are important – linked with Darwinian artifice to each other and to "widows" by means of alliteration. Winking is the imaginative act of comic irony, a step toward the will-o-the-wisp supreme fiction that can never be reached, and it is turned on and stimulated by the shock and despair of wincing. Finally, nothing is definite except the playful, manipulative talk between the poet and the widow. Man is alone with his mental activity, his animal motion. This is the supreme fiction.

Stevens' poetry is preoccupied with aesthetics. Many of his poems are simply about the poetic activity and its self-sufficient meaning. In the sense that Darwin discovers and describes imaginative motion as being incapable of "meaning" anything at the same time that it is our most powerful animal motion – giving us the most vivid "illusion" of meaning, of being alive – Stevens also celebrates the power of the imagination.

---

[10] My knowledge of Stevens is not a very scholarly knowledge although I did do my honors paper on him at Williams College. Since that time, my scholarship has been mostly on earlier literature. It was a genuine pleasure, however, to read through Stevens again when the analogy to Darwin suggested itself.

[11] Wallace Stevens, *Harmonium* (New York: Alfred Knopf, 1953), p. 101. "A High-Toned Old Christian Woman."

It is the fabulous power of intensified, recombined perception, of colors and fat seeds. The following passage about the aesthetic of the poet, Crispin, in "The Comedian as the Letter C" reminds me both of Darwin's theorizing about imaginative motion and also of the thick texture of his verse itself:

> ... beautiful barenesses as yet unseen,
> Making the most of savagery of palms,
> Of moonlight on the thick, cadaverous bloom
> That yuccas breed, and of the panther's tread.
> The fabulous and its intrinsic verse
> Came like two spirits parleying, adorned
> In radiance from the Atlantic coign,
> For Crispin and his quill to catechize.
> But they came parleying of such an earth,
> So thick with sides and jagged lops of green,
> So intertwinted with serpent-kin encoiled
> Among the purple tufts, the scarlet crowns,
> Scenting the jungle in their refuges,
> So streaked with yellow, blue and green and red
> In beak and bud and fruity gobbet-skins,
> That earth was like a jostling festival
> Of seeds grown fat, too juicily opulent,
> Expanding in the gold's maternal warmth.[12]

The fecundity of imaginative motion, however, even though it cannot give us any strict analogies about the natural world is very similar to the fecundity of all motion in the universe. Thus when Stevens or Darwin celebrates the fecundity of imagination, they are also celebrating the fecundity of all motion. Such motion is not necessarily friendly to individual human beings, as we have seen, and so to recognize and to accept it produces the clutch of despair, the "wincing." But the power is with the motion, and paradoxically the only human thing to do is to give up the old illusions about an anthropocentric universe (or rather use them as imaginative motions) and to accept the motions.

For the poet this means accepting the role of minor poet. There are many more than nine muses, all tentative. Similarly, the philosopher and the scientist must accept tentativeness and uncertainty in a moving world. All imaginative and animal motions have something absurd about them at the same time that they are all we have. Stevens ends his poem

---

[12] *Ibid.,* p. 55. "The Comedian as the Letter C."

about the imaginative Crispin with a passage that in an uncanny way
seems to characterize the stubborn, gay, stuttering Darwin:

> ... if Crispin is a profitless
> Philosopher, beginning with green brag,
> Concluding fadedly, if as a man
> Prone to distemper he abates in taste,
> Fickle and fumbling, variable, obscure,
> Glozing his life with after-shining flicks,
> Illuminating, from a fancy gorged
> By Apparition, plain and common things,
> Sequestering the fluster from the year,
> Making gulped potions from obstreperous drops,
> And so distorting, proving what he proves
> Is nothing, what can all this matter since
> The relation comes, benignly, to its end?
> So may the relation of each man be clipped.[13]

What redeems all this is motion. Nothing is ever finally "clipped." And
in the particular case of Erasmus Darwin, who clipped off many relations
– fourteen children including the father of Charles Darwin, several
fascinating if imperfect books, and innumerable theories whose seed-
time may not yet be over – the initial energy should not be forgotten.

[13] *Ibid.*, pp. 77-78. "The Comedian as the Letter C."

BIBLIOGRAPHICAL LIST

Adler, Jacob H. *The Reach of Art*: *A Study in the Prosody Of Pope*. Gainsville: University of Florida Press, 1964.

Arnheim, Rudolf. *Entropy and Art*: *An Essay on Disorder and Order*. Berkeley and Los Angeles: University of California Press, 1971.

Ashmun, Margaret. *The Singing Swan*. 1931; rpt. New York: Greenwood Press, 1968.

Ault, Donald D. *Visionary Physics*: *Blake's Response to Newton*. Diss. University of Chicago 1970.

Bate, Walter Jackson. "The English Poet and the Burden of the Past, 1660-1820." *Aspects of the Eighteenth Century*. Ed. Earl R. Wasserman. Baltimore: Johns Hopkins Press, 1965.

Bedford, John. *Wedgwood Jasper Ware*. New York: Walter and Co., 1964.

Blackstone, Bernard. *The Consecrated Urn*: *An Interpretation of Keats in Terms of Growth and Form*. London: Longmans, Green, 1959.

Boyd, John D. *The Function of Mimesis and Its Decline*. Cambridge: Harvard Univ. Press, 1968.

Braudy, Leo. "*Fanny Hill* and Materialism." *Eighteenth-Century Studies*, 4 (Fall, 1970), 21-40.

Bronson, Bertrand H. "Postscript Rasselas." *Samuel Johnson, Rasselas, Poems, and Selected Prose*. San Francisco: Rinehart, 1971.

Boswell, James. *Life of Johnson*. 1971; rpt. London: Oxford Univ. Press, 1904.

Burke, Edmund. *A Philosophical Enquiry into the Origin of Our Ideas of the Sublime and Beautiful*. Ed. J. T. Boulton. 1756; rpt. Notre Dame: University of Notre Dame Press, 1968.

Clark, Ronald W. *Einstein*: *The Life and Times*. New York: World, 1971.

Clifford, James L. *Young Sam Johnson*. New York: McGraw-Hill, 1955.

Cohen, I. Bernard. *Franklin and Newton*. Philadelphia American Philosophical Society, 1956.

Coleridge, Samuel Taylor. *Collected Letters of . . . .* Ed. Earl Leslie Griggs. Oxford: Clarendon Press, 1956.

Darwin, Charles. "Preliminary Notice." *Erasmus Darwin*. Ernst Krause. London: John Murray, 1879.

Darwin, Erasmus. *The Essential Writings of . . . .* Ed. Desmond King-Hele. London: MacGibbon & Kee, 1968.

—. *The Botanic Garden, Part I*. London: J. Johnson, 1791.

—. *The Botanic Garden, Part II.* 4th edition, London: J. Johnson, 1799.

—. *The Botanic Garden: A Poem, in Two Parts.* 2nd American edition, New York: T. & J. Swords, 1807.

—. *The Temple of Nature; or, The Origin of Society: A Poem, With Philosophical Notes.* London: J. Johnson, 1803.

—. *The Temple of Nature: or, The Origin of Society: A Poem, With Philosophical Notes.* New York: T. & J. Swords, 1804.

—. *Zoonomia; or, The Laws of Organic Life.* vol. I, London: J. Johnson, 1794. vol. II, London: J. Johnson, 1796.

—. *Zoonomia; or, The Laws of Organic Life.* vol. I, New York: T. & J. Swords, 1796, vol. II, Philadelphia: T. Dobson, 1797.

Davie, Donald. "John Ledyard; The American Traveler and his Sentimental Journeys." *Eighteenth-Century Studies,* 4 (Fall, 1970), 57-70.

de Beer, Sir Gavin. *Charles Darwin: A Scientific Biography.* 1963; rpt. New York: Doubleday Anchor, 1965.

Durrant, Geoffrey. *Wordsworth and the Great System.* New York: Cambridge Univ. Press, 1970.

Erdman, David V., ed. *The Poetry and Prose of William Blake.* New York: Doubleday, 1965.

Frye, Northrop. "Towards Defining an Age of Sensibility." *Fables of Identity: Studies in Poetic Mythology.* New York: Harbinger, 1963.

Fussell, Paul, Jr. *Poetic Meter and Poetic Form.* New York: Random House, 1965.

—. *Theory of Prosody in Eighteenth-Century England.* New London: Connecticut College, 1954.

Gillispie, Charles Coulston. *The Edge of Objectivity: An Essay in the History of Scientific Ideas.* Princeton: Princeton Univ. Press, 1960.

Gray, Thomas. *Gray's Poems, Letters, and Essays.* Eds. John Drinkwater and Lewis Gibbs. New York: Dutton, 1912.

Hagstrum, Jean. "Gray's Sensibility." unpublished paper read at Carleton University, May 18, 1971.

Hagstrum, Jean. *Samuel Johnson's Literary Criticism.* 1952; rpt. Chicago: University of Chicago Press, 1967.

Hagstrum, Jean H. *The Sister Arts.* Chicago: University of Chicago Press, 1958.

Hassler, Donald Mackey. *The Poems of Erasmus Darwin.* Diss. Columbia University 1967.

Haynes, D. E. L. *The Portland Vase.* London: The British Museum, 1964.

Hume, David. *Essential Works of . . . .* Ed. Ralph Cohen. New York: Bantam Books, 1965.

Hunt, John Dixon. "Emblem and Expressionism in the Eighteenth-Century Landscape Garden." *Eighteenth-Century Studies,* 4 (Spring, 1971), 294-317.

Hussey, Christopher. *The Picturesque: Studies in a Point of View: With a New Preface by the Author.* 1927; rpt. Hamden: Archon Books, 1967.

Jack, Ian. *Keats and the Mirror of Art.* Oxford: Oxford Univ. Press, 1967.

King-Hele, Desmond. *Erasmus Darwin, 1731-1802.* London: Macmillan, 1963.

La Mettrie, Julien. *Man a Machine. The Age of Enlightenment.* Ed. Lester G. Crocker. New York: Harper & Row, 1969.

Lemon, Lee T. and Marion J. Reis, eds. *Russian Formalist Criticism: Four Essays.* Lincoln: University of Nebraska Press, 1965.

Lipking, Lawrence. *The Ordering of the Arts in Eighteenth-Century England.* Princeton: Princeton Univ. Press, 1970.

Logan, James V. *The Poetry and Aesthetics of Erasmus Darwin.* Princeton: Princeton Univ. Press, 1936.

Mack, Maynard. *The Garden and the City: Retirement and Politics in the Later Poetry of Pope 1731-1743.* Toronto: University of Toronto Press, 1969.

Manwaring, Elizabeth Wheeler. *Italian Landscape in Eighteenth Century England: A Study Chiefly of the Influence of Claude Lorrain and Salvator Rosa on English Taste 1700-1800.* New York: Oxford Univ. Press, 1925.

Mitchell, W. J. T. "Poetic and Pictorial Imagination in Blake's *The Book of Urizen.*" *Eighteenth-Century Studies,* 3 (Fall, 1969), 83-107.

Mossner, Ernest Campbell. *The Life of David Hume.* 1954; rpt. Oxford: Clarendon Press, 1970.

Newton, Sir Issac. *Opticks.* Ed. I. Bernard Cohen. 4th edition. 1730; rpt. New York: Dover, 1952.

Pearson, Hesketh. *Doctor Darwin.* New York: Walker & Co., 1963.

Perkins, David. *Wordsworth and the Poetry of Sincerity.* Cambridge: Harvard Univ. Press, 1964.

Popkin, Richard H. "David Hume: His Pyrrhonism and His Critique of Pyrrhonism." *Hume.* Ed. V. C. Chappell. Notre Dame: Univ. of Notre Dame Press, 1968.

Price, Martin. "The Picturesque Moment." *From Sensibility to Romanticism.* Eds. Frederick W. Hilles and Harold Bloom. New York: Oxford Univ. Press, 1965.

Priestley, Joseph. *Memoirs.* Ed. John T. Boyer. 1806; rpt. Washington: Barcroft Press, 1964.

Primer, Irwin. "Erasmus Darwin's *Temple of Nature*: Progress, Evolution, and Eleusinian Mysteries." *Journal of the History of Ideas,* 25 (Jan. March 1964), 58-76.

Ransom, John Crowe. "The Strange Music of English Verse." *Kenyon Review,* 18 (Summer, 1956), 460-477.

Roe, Albert S. "The Thunder of Egypt: Blake and Erasmus Darwin." *William Blake: Essays for S. Foster Damon.* Ed. Alvin H. Rosenfeld. Providence: Brown Univ. Press, 1969.

Ross, Robert N. " 'To Charm Thy Curious Eye': Erasmus Darwin's Poetry at the Vestibule of Knowledge." *Journal of the History of Ideas,* 32 (July-Sept. 1971), 379-394.

Rousseau, G. S. "Science and the Discovery of the Imagination in Enlightened England." *Eighteenth-Century Studies,* 3 (Fall, 1969), 108-135.

Schneider, Elisabeth. *Coleridge, Opium and Kubla Khan.* Chicago: Univ. of Chicago Press, 1953.

Schofield, Robert E. *The Lunar Society of Birmingham.* Oxford: Oxford Univ. Press, 1963.

—. *Mechanism and Materialism: British Natural Philosophy in an Age of Reason.* Princeton: Princeton Univ. Press, 1970.

Seward, Anna. *The Letters of* . . . . Edinburgh, 1811.

—. *Memoirs of the Life of Dr. Darwin.* London: J. Johnson, 1804.

Sewell, Elizabeth. *The Orphic Voice: Poetry and Natural History.* New Haven: Yale Univ. Press, 1960.

Sister Miriam Joseph. *Rhetoric in Shakespeare's Time.* New York: Harcourt Brace, 1962.

Steen, Lynn Arthur. "New Models of the Real-Number Line." *Scientific American,* 225 (August 1971), 92-99.

Stevens, Wallace. *Harmonium*. 1923; rpt. New York: Knopf, 1953.

—. *Opus Posthumous*. Ed. Samuel French Morse. New York: Knopf, 1957.

Tillotson, Geoffrey. *Augustan Poetic Diction*. London: The Athlone Press, 1964.

Vartanian, Aram. *La Mettrie's l'Homme machine: A Study in the Origins of an Idea*. Princeton: Princeton University Press, 1960.

Vorzimmer, Peter J. *Charles Darwin: The Years of Controversy*. Philadelphia: Temple Univ. Press, 1970.

Wallerstein, Ruth. "The Development of the Rhetoric and Metre of the Heroic Couplet, Especially in 1726-1945." *Essential Articles for the Study of English Augustan Backgrounds*. Ed. Bernard N. Schilling. Hamden: Shoe String Press, 1961.

Walpole, Horace. *The Letters of* .... Ed. Mrs. Paget Toynbee. Oxford: Oxford Univ. Press, 1905.

Wellek, Rene and Austin Warren. *Theory of Literature*. 3rd edition. 1942; rpt. New York: Harcourt Brace, 1962.

Wimsatt, W. K. *Hateful Contraries*. Lexington: Univ. of Kentucky, 1965.

—. *The Verbal Icon: Studies in the Meaning of Poetry*. New York: Noonday Press, 1965.

Wimsatt, W. K. and Monroe C. Beardsley. "The Concept of Meter: An Exercise in Abstraction." *PMLA*, 74 (1959), 585-598.

INDEX

Addison, Joseph, 38
Adler, Jacob, 73
aesthetic school of the Whartons, 35
Arnheim, Rudolf, 54n
Ashmun, Margaret, 16–17
Ault, Donald D., 12n

bar-foot analogists, 65
Baretti, Joseph, 1
Bate, Walter Jackson, 6–8, 15, 21
Beardsley, Monroe, 63
Beattie, James, 15–16
Bedford, John, 51n
Blackstone, Bernard, 84n
Blake, William, 45–46
Boerhaave, Herman, 24–25
Boothby, Sir Brooke, 54
Boswell, James, 16, 18
Boyd, John D., S.J., 13, 26
Bronson, Bertrand H., 1n
Bryant, Jacob, 49
Burke, Edmund, 52, 58
Byron, Lord, 48, 76, 87

camera obscura, 45
Cannon, Walter F., 1n
Cheyne and "The English Malady," 17–
   18
chiasmus, 73–74, 86–89
circularity, 86–89
Clark, Ronald W., 24n
Cohen, I. Bernard, 12n, 23n
Coleridge, S. T., viii, 4–5, 7, 26, 34–35, 48,
   64, 66

comic materialism, 20–22, 41
comic tone, 75–80, 89–92

Danet, Pierre, 49
Darwin, Charles, vii, 19, 92
DARWIN, ERASMUS: works
   The Botanic Garden, 4, 24, 38, 44, 50–
      51, 59, 83, 86–87
   "The Death of Prince Frederick," 4
   "The Economy of Vegetation," 54, 66,
      69, 75, 83, 89
   "The Loves of the Plants," 36–37, 41–
      42, 45, 47, 54, 65, 68, 73–74, 83, 87
   Phytologia, 83
   The Temple of Nature, 29n, 30n, 31–32,
      49–50, 54–55, 59, 66, 82–83, 87
   Zoonomia, 4, 7–8, 10, 19, 24, 27, 28, 35,
      53, 55, 56
Darwin, Robert, 19

Einstein, Albert, 24n
Eleusinian mysteries, 49–52, 54, 82
epistemology, 11–14
European Magazine, 4

Fanny Hill, 56
Formalism, Russian literary, 62
formalist criticism, 61–63
Franklin, Benjamin, 13–14, 24, 27, 28
Freud, Sigmund, 53
Frye, Northrop, 21
Fuseli, Henry, 45–47, 49, 52
Fussell, Paul, 64–65, 70